INDIA'S GREATEST REFORMERS

Dr K.L. Johar got his bachelor's degree from Panjab University, Chandigarh, in 1957 and later his master's and PhD degrees in English literature from Meerut University (now Chaudhary Charan Singh University, Meerut).

After working for over 30 years as lecturer and principal of Mukand Lal National College, Yamunanagar, he was appointed as pro-vice-chancellor of Kurukshetra University. Later, he joined as the founder vice chancellor of Guru Jambheswar University of Science & Technology, Hisar, in 1995 and brought about many educational reforms.

Dr Johar has written extensively on the freedom movement. His books *Martyr Bhagat Singh: An Intimate View*, *Ajit Singh (Uncle of Martyr Bhagat Singh): An Exiled Revolutionary*, *Relevance of Subhas Bose Today*, *Private Initiatives in Higher Education* and *Eminent Women Freedom Fighters of India: Profiles in Courage and Conviction* have been widely acclaimed.

Dr Johar brought out three books on the freedom movement during the Amrit Mahotsav in 2022. He produced a book, *Uttar Bharat Ke Swatantrata Senani*, at the request of Speaker, Uttar Pradesh Vidhan Sabha. It was released on 13 June 2023.

INDIA'S GREATEST REFORMERS

51
EXTRAORDINARY STORIES

K.L. JOHAR

RUPA

Published by
Rupa Publications India Pvt. Ltd 2024
7/16, Ansari Road, Daryaganj
New Delhi 110002

Sales centres:
Bengaluru Chennai
Hyderabad Jaipur Kathmandu
Calcutta Mumbai Prayagraj

P-ISBN: 978-93-6156-773-5
E-ISBN: 978-93-6156-536-6

First impression 2024

10 9 8 7 6 5 4 3 2 1

Printed in India

To my revered mother, Smt. Ishar Devi, who, despite her own financial constraints, performed the marriage ceremony of her domestic help's daughter at her own residence in Yamunanagar.

To the thousands of social reformers in the country who immortalized themselves by rendering acts of charity and compassion and through eradication of malpractices from Indian society.

To Prof. Tilak Raj Chhadha, a veteran freedom fighter and an educationist, my guru, guide and philosopher who shaped me to become what I am today.

CONTENTS

FOREWORD

I am privileged and honoured to have been asked to write the foreword to this book authored by Dr K.L. Johar, writer of many books on freedom movement including *Martyr Bhagat Singh: An Intimate View*, *Relevance of Subhas Bose Today* and *Eminent Women Freedom Fighters of India: Profiles in Courage and Conviction*. What convinced me to write this foreword were the names of the 51 illustrious social reformers—including Raja Ram Mohan Roy and Ishwar Chandra Vidyasagar, who transformed the social structure of India with their contribution towards abolition of sati and legalization of widow remarriage respectively, in the middle of the nineteenth century.

Then we have Mahatma Gandhi and Dr B.R. Ambedkar, who made concrete efforts to remove the black stain of untouchability from Indian society. Likewise, Subhas Bose did a miraculous job by starting a common kitchen for all communities—including Hindus, Muslims, Christians and Sikhs—in his Azad Hind Fauj (Indian National Army) in Southeast Asia.

In contemporary India, Kailash Satyarthi, a Nobel laureate, has dedicated his life to eradicating child labour and promoting children's rights to education and protection. Dr Bindeshwar Pathak is the founder of Sulabh International, an organization working towards improving sanitation and hygiene conditions for millions of Indians. He has set up more than 2 million *sulabh sauchalayas* and around 10,000 'pay and use' toilets in the urban areas. His effort to stop open defecation is commendable. Devendra Raj Mehta is another luminary who has helped with prosthetic foot and other artificial limb fitments for about 25 lakh persons suffering from one or the other physical disability. Through his social effort he has brought smiles on the faces of millions of people, not only in India but also in 41 other countries, by holding over 100 camps.

My mother, Bibi Amar Kaur (sister of Shaheed Bhagat Singh), would take me to Amritsar to meet Bhagat Puran Singh, who would be sitting at the doors of the Golden Temple with his adopted sons and daughters who were unfortunately abandoned by their parents for being physically challenged and mentally underdeveloped. His service to humanity was always an inspiration to me as a young boy. It taught me that true religious practice was the service being done by Bhagat Puran Singh. He would distribute literature printed on reused paper and it would be rich with valuable stories. This would inspire everyone to serve the community. He would inspire others to be careful about resources and nature. I find a glimpse of his story narrated in this book.

As many as 18 women social activists find their rightful place in this book. Notable among them are Bilkees Idrees Latif, who put her own life in danger to douse the flames of communal frenzy in Bombay in 1980; Daya Bai, a Christian missionary who helped the tribal population in Madhya Pradesh; Janaki Devi Bajaj, a rich woman who gave all her gold and jewellery for the freedom movement, promoted khadi and picketed liquor shops; Mary Clubwala Jadhav, an enlightened Parsi who, through her Guild of Service, nursed the wounded soldiers with her own hands. There are also names like Mother Teresa—known for her care of the sick, the elderly and the orphans around the globe—who later became a Nobel laureate and got canonized as a saint; Dr Shantha Sinha, who changed the shape of Andhra Pradesh by helping young children working as domestic help; and Usha Chaumar, who started her life as a manual scavenger collecting excreta from house to house, and later became an entrepreneur and then the president of Sulabh International in Rajasthan.

Thus, the book is a fine combination of men and women who—through their acts of social reform—did a commendable job in their times in the eighteenth, nineteenth and twentieth centuries, and also in contemporary India. In the initial phase, it will be seen that India was fighting a grim battle for freedom. Lakhs of people were incarcerated and faced British atrocities. The revolutionaries like Shaheed Bhagat Singh, Ram Prasad Bismil and Chandra Shekhar Azad, along with hundreds of companions, played a stellar role in this struggle. Around the same time, there were crusaders of social reform of the stature of Raja Ram Mohan Roy, Keshab Chandra Sen and Ishwar Chandra Vidyasagar who were fighting the existing social order to eradicate the prevailing evil practices.

On the other hand, in contemporary India after Independence, the nature of social reforms underwent a change. It related to child education, environment and making all-out efforts to bring about an egalitarian society. Persons like Anil Prakash Joshi, a prominent environmentalist from Uttarakhand; Sunderlal Bahuguna, famous for his 'Chipko Andolan'; Kailash Satyarthi, a child education activist; D.R. Mehta and Dr Uma Tuli, who worked for persons with disabilities; and many more who raised the issues of rape, sexual assault, and exploitation by the rich also came to the fore.

It should be noted here that a country like the United States (US), which gloats about being the greatest democracy in the world, could abolish slavery from their land only in 1865 with the bold steps taken by Abraham Lincoln, the sixteenth president. Martin Luther King, Jr, an iconic figure in the American Civil Rights Movement, played an instrumental role in advocating for racial equality in the US. But in his crusade against inequality he was assassinated in 1968, just at the age of 39. Nelson Mandela, an iconic leader of South Africa, suffered in jail for 27 years before he could put an end to apartheid in South Africa in 1994. It can thus be seen that social activists around the globe have made sacrifices and suffered innumerable hardships in their lives to improve the quality of life for the citizens of their respective countries. India has been no exception. After all, Dayanand Saraswati, founder of the Arya Samaj, was poisoned to death; and later Mahatma Gandhi was assassinated primarily because he was working for communal harmony.

Dr K.L. Johar has written pen-portraits of 51 social activists who shone as stars in the firmament. These individuals have inspired generations and will continue to inspire future generations as well. I am sure the efforts of Dr K.L. Johar is worthy of praise, as India continues to be haunted by many social evils even 75 years after Independence. While I congratulate the author, I dedicate this book to the readers who will find it not only interesting and enlightening, but also very inspiring.

—Prof. Jagmohan Singh*
Secretary, Shaheed Bhagat Singh Research Committee (Regd.)

*Prof. Jagmohan Singh is the nephew of Shaheed Bhagat Singh and has researched and written extensively on him.

INTRODUCTION

The idea of writing a book on social reformers of India came to my mind when going through the pages of history relating to the freedom movement. I found that the people of India, by and large, were used to a life of servitude under the British rule. They had developed a slavish frame of mind and thought they would never get out of it. Things were no better in other parts of the world. For instance, there was a time in the United States when black people were sold like articles of daily use. Such a black man would become the property of the buyer. He had no will of his own. He danced to his master's tune.

In the United Kingdom, where the rulers boasted of having sway over 56 countries, autocracy prevailed most of the time. Voting rights were given for a democratic government only in 1918, although some persons belonging to the rich and influential categories had this privilege as early as 1832. In South Africa, which was a colony of the Britishers, voting rights were granted only in 1994. Sometimes, one imagines that one was living in a world of savages where might was right. The apartheid practised in South Africa is a glaring example of atrocious behaviour towards humanity.

It is, however, believed that civilizations and civilized people thrived in the ancient period. The Indus Valley Civilization came about in 3300 to 2500 BCE and spread to other parts of the world. People then were rich and prosperous. There was art, culture and civilization. For example, a Sanskrit scholar of the status of Kalidasa was in the court of the Gupta period in India and produced rich literature that finds no match even today. Chandragupta Maurya and Ashoka 'The Great' have been considered as great emperors. Buddhism and Jainism flourished in these times.

The inception of the Mughal Empire in 1526 produced kings like Akbar. But then there was Aurangzeb and others, under whom it was a period of grave social injustice. There were forcible conversions, and places of worship of the Hindus were demolished. After the Battle of Plassey in 1757, the East India Company (EIC) held sway over most of the principalities. But Great Britain took control in 1858 and ruled for about 90 years until India became free in 1947. The major problem during these 90 years was to find ways and means to demolish the British edifice to free India. Many leaders came forward for this. Mahatma Gandhi, Pandit (Pt) Jawaharlal Nehru, Govind Ballabh Pant and thousands of others raised their voices. But these voices were stifled. The revolutionaries played a stellar role during this time. Bhagat Singh, Chandra Shekhar Azad, Ram Prasad Bismil and many others waged an armed struggle against the British and were martyred. As lakhs of people languished in jails, the priority was the attainment of freedom. Therefore, acts of social reform were relegated to the background.

In this era of rule by the EIC, and later by Great Britain, the people of India suffered untold miseries and hardships. On the one hand, there were stalwarts who struggled for freedom from the British, and on the other, there were gritty and determined social reformers who undertook various acts of social reform with regards to sati, untouchability, liquor consumption, sexual assaults, environmental hazards and many other such evils.

Social reformers like Raja Ram Mohan Roy and Ishwar Chandra Vidyasagar, both nineteenth-century stalwarts, could not bear the evil social practices rampant in their times. For example, the practice of sati prevailed. Young widows were forced to burn themselves on the pyre of their dead husbands. Child marriage was also in vogue and widow remarriage was disallowed. There was no education worth its name and sexual assault was a common practice. The rich landlords looked upon the depressed classes as slaves and bonded labourers.

Social reformers waged a different type of battle from those engaged in the freedom movement. Their battle was two-fold. One was to fight the Brahminical thought which stood by these evil practices, and the other was to persuade the British rulers to help put an end to these practices. The social reformers wrote in newspapers and journals, and faced stiff resistance in the prevailing social order. Unmindful of criticism, Raja Ram Mohan Roy and Ishwar Chandra Vidyasagar respectively persuaded William Bentinck and Lord Dalhousie to abolish sati and to allow widow remarriage by acts of legislation in 1829 and 1856.

In the twentieth century, Mahatma Gandhi and B.R. Ambedkar emerged as champions to eradicate untouchability, particularly manual scavenging. Swami Vivekananda raised his voice against the caste system. Many others also came forward and spoke for khadi cottage industry and women's education, and against liquor consumption.

In contemporary India, other areas of social activism have gripped the mind of individuals. Kailash Satyarthi waged a struggle against the suppression of children and young people, and fought for children's education. He was awarded the coveted Nobel Prize for his unrelenting struggle. Earlier, Vinoba Bhave had measured the length and breadth of the country for his

Bhoodan Movement. He had collected around 45 lakh acres of land and distributed the same among landless labourers. Mary Clubwala Jadhav worked throughout her life through her Guild of Service for girls' education, and Sindhutai Sapkal established orphanages all over the country. Bhagat Puran Singh shot into fame on the strength of his Pingalwara Movement. Prem Singh, an audit officer with the Government of India, sold his all to look after the leprosy patients in Punjab. Similarly, Baba Amte from Maharashtra was the champion for the cause of leprosy patients. Another person in this category was Swami Sivananda from Varanasi (previously Banaras).

Dr Bindeshwar Pathak, in his effort to put an end to open defecation, built around 2 million *sulabh sauchalaya*s across the country and worked with zeal and enthusiasm even at the age of 80. In a personal interview, Devendra Raj Mehta, a retired bureaucrat, revealed that he had provided artificial limbs to more than 25 million people across the globe. He has gone to over 41 countries where he held more than 100 foot-fitment camps. Dr Uma Tuli, through her Amar Jyoti Charitable Trust in New Delhi, takes care of specially-abled children in her school and has greatly served the cause of the disabled.

The 51 pen-portraits given by me in this book come from various states of India. All of them have done great work in their times for the eradication of social evils in the country. I became richer by reading and writing about them. It was an experience filled with pleasure and pain. It was full of pleasure because I came across personalities who were in a class by themselves—they stood tall and colossal. It was painful, as finding the facts about them was a very difficult exercise. Although my secretary, Smt. Kusum Karki, browsed the net and found out many articles on them, some help still had to be taken from National Archives of India and the national libraries. Additionally, I held personal interviews with some of the crusaders of social reform.

Overall, I am glad that I took up the exercise, as it has given me great satisfaction. I hope my readers will take inspiration from the life stories of the great men and women of India who, amid the toil and tumble of the freedom movement, pooled their energies and brought about acts of social justice. Their work has surely changed the quality of life in India.

However, if we start believing that all is well with Indian society, we are gravely mistaken. There is still a gender bias. Even now, only 15 per cent of the members of Lok Sabha are women. Untouchability is still practised in some parts of the country, and tribals continue to live a life of abject misery. The gap between the rich and the poor is widening. There are social, economic and political disparities. Much of this can be fixed only with the political will of the government in power. But no one can deny that in British-ruled India, and now in free India, many stalwarts have worked and are working for improvement in the quality of life of the people by helping eliminate social evils. As an author, I salute them and hope that many more, in the government or outside it will follow in their footsteps.

ANIL PRAKASH JOSHI

The Mountain Man

Dr Anil Prakash Joshi—popularly known as 'The Mountain Man' and conferred with a plethora of awards—has done commendable work in the field of environmental ecology. He is a household name in Uttarakhand. He gave up a comfortable and lucrative job as a reader in the Dr P.D.B. Himalayan Government Post Graduate College, Kotdwar, in 1979, and engaged himself in the onerous task of helping rural men and women through his research work. His work has won him the gratitude of the nation, as he has rendered considerable help to the rural Uttarakhand community, particularly the womenfolk in the area.

He was born on 6 April 1955 in Kotdwar, Pauri Garhwal, in Uttarakhand. After his early education in the village, he did his master's degree in botany and later got a PhD in ecology from Garhwal University. Although he joined the teaching profession in a government college, his mind seemed to lay elsewhere. He made up his mind to apply his knowledge in the service of humanity. With a group of 30 more research fellows, he moved about in the hilly areas of Uttarakhand. He founded the Himalayan Environmental Studies and Conservation Organization in 1979. His focus was two-fold: the first was environmental conservation, and the second to explore avenues for self-employment. He achieved incredible success in both areas.

He and his friends developed new environment-friendly technologies to help the farmers. He undertook the task of disseminating knowledge about what the farmers could gain by making use of these technologies. For example, he told them about a shrub which was discarded as a weed. It is also called *kurri* in local parlance. He came up with the idea that this shrub could be used in making furniture and incense sticks, and the leftover portion could be used as fodder. This provided self-employment to thousands of women and at the same time a shrub, which was earlier thrown away as a weed, was put to considerable use.

Similarly, he advised the villagers that the *prasad* (offerings) distributed in temples could be made out of local grains. His contact with the Vaishno Devi Shrine was useful as the prasad distributed there is now made from grains grown in the fields of the farmers. This is also used in the Badrinath, Kedarnath, Yamunotri, and Gangotri temples as well as hundreds of other temples in Uttarakhand.

Dr Joshi rejuvenated hundreds of springs and streams in the Himalayan sand. The water flowing from these springs and streams could be used for irrigation in the fields. His concept of 'gross environmental product' (GEP) was recognized by the state government on 5 June 2021. He coined GEP as an ecological growth measure parallel to GDP.

Dr Joshi has worked on many other projects such as Women Technology Park, Ecological Food Mission in Mountain and Women's Initiative for Self Employment. He has successfully provided the villages with water mills, composting pits, toilets, plan-based drugs, herbal pesticides and rainwater harvesting techniques. In fact, he even gave a slogan, 'Local need meet locally.'[1] The people of Uttarakhand look upon him as someone who has given them a new ray of hope. The rural people have benefitted greatly from his technologies.

The nation as a whole is proud of the man who has developed a technology with far-reaching consequences. His services have been recognized at all levels. He is considered a great social reformer. He has been conferred with many awards including the Jamnalal Bajaj Award in 2006 for his rural development programmes. The same year he was conferred with the fourth highest civilian award, Padma Shri, by the Government of India. He received the Jawaharlal Nehru Award from the Indian Science Congress in 1999. To top it all, he received the Padma Bhushan—the third highest civilian award—in 2020 for environmental conservation in Uttarakhand. He has been named an Ashoka Fellow. Ashoka is a United States-based nonprofit organization that promotes social entrepreneurship by connecting and supporting individual social entrepreneurs.

---

[1]'Dr. Anil Prakash Joshi', *Passion Vista,* https://tinyurl.com/yc7mvx3h. Accessed on 7 March 2024.

B.R. AMBEDKAR

The Fight for Equality

A victim of indignity, humiliation and ignominy in the initial years of his life, Bhimrao Ramji (B.R.) Ambedkar waged an unrelenting crusade against the caste practice prevalent in India. Simply because he belonged to the Mahar community—considered to be low in status and untouchable—he was humiliated both by his teachers and classmates in his school in Satara, Maharashtra. He would be made to sit outside the class on a gunny bag he had brought from home. He would not be allowed the facility of drinking water from the same tap as the students belonging to upper castes.

He suffered all this and much more with a sense of patience and fortitude. But the malice of the caste system and the subsequent humiliation was sinking deep in his mind. He nourished aspirations and dreams that were both social and academic in nature. Therefore, he took all that happened to him and those like him in stride and moved ahead.

B.R. Ambedkar was born on 14 April 1891 at Mhow (now in Madhya Pradesh) to Ramji and Bhima Devi. While Ramji was a subedar in the British Army, Bhima Devi was a devout religious woman. He was hardly three years old when his father retired from service in the Army. The family then moved to Satara in Maharashtra.

Ambedkar graduated from Elphinstone College, Bombay (now Mumbai)—an institute reputed for its academic excellence. He joined service with the Baroda state government. On the strength of his scholarship and merit, he was selected for a stipend by Sayajirao Gaekwad III of Baroda to study in Columbia University, United States. He had completed his master's and PhD degrees by 1916. His subject for the PhD thesis was 'National Dividend for India—A Historic and Analytical Study'. Later, he moved to London where he studied in the London School of Economics (LSE) and simultaneously joined Gray's Inn for a degree in law. He studied for some time in the University of Bonn, Germany, as well.

Post that, he returned to India for a brief duration, as his tenure for scholarship had ended. He then took up a couple of jobsbut ended up getting fired, being considered an 'untouchable' even though he was very popular among the students of Sydenham College of Commerce and Economics, Bombay. At this point, the Maharaja of Kolhapur gave him a scholarship, and he went back to London to take up his degree in law and also his DSc degree from LSE.

It can be asserted that B.R. Ambedkar was the most qualified man of India in the 1920s. The treatment meted out to persons from depressed classes at that time was appalling. The hegemony of the Hindus and Brahmins reigned supreme. The caste system, as sanctioned by the Hindu scripture Manusmriti, was in vogue. The Congress party, then under the leadership of Mahatma Gandhi, was doing very little to redress the grievances of the depressed classes.

It was in such a scenario that Ambedkar emerged on the scene. He set up an association for the welfare of the depressed classes, with Sir Chimanlal Setalvad as president. He also set up the Bahishkrit Hitakarini Sabha. He gave vent to his anger and indignation through various weekly newspapers like *Mooknayak, Bahishkrit Bharat* and *Equality Janta*. These papers carried fiery articles against inequality and social injustice. He was now looked upon as a *maseeha* (saviour) of the depressed classes. As a mark of respect, he was called 'Babasaheb' Bhimrao Ambedkar.

Ambedkar firmly believed that the Manusmriti was the root cause of the caste system in India. This division, according to him, was an unholy act. God had created all beings as equal. There was no question of low and high. Therefore, he, with thousands of his followers, burnt copies of the Manusmriti on 25 December 1927. The upper-caste Hindus thought it to be an act of sacrilege and hurled abuses at Ambedkar. But he was on a steady course and moved on the path which he thought was righteous. He never, even for a moment, wavered in his resolve to remove the stigma of the caste system from the face of India.

Under these circumstances, Ambedkar was up in arms against the Congress party. The British government recognized his talent, merit and capacity for work, and invited him to all the three round-table conferences held in London in the early 1930s as a representative of the depressed classes. Gandhi ji looked at it as a ruse by the British authorities to divide the Hindu society. He declared, 'The interests of the untouchables are as dear to the Congress as the interests of any other body or of any other individual throughout the length and breadth of India. Therefore, I would most strongly resist any further representation.'[1]

But Ambedkar thought differently and advanced arguments to prove that the Congress party, or its leader, Gandhi, could not

---

[1]Roy Choudhury, P.C., *Gandhi and His Contemporaries*, Sterling Publishers, 2008.

represent the depressed classes in the meetings. He said, 'But I would like to make this matter absolutely plain at the start. Those who are negotiating ought to understand that they are not plenipotentiaries at all; that whatever may be the representative character of Mr. Gandhi or the Congress people, they certainly are not in a position to bind us—certainly not. I say that most emphatically in this meeting.'[2]

As a result of the round-table conferences in London, the British government in India came up with its 'Communal Award' on 16 August 1932, which meant that there would be separate seats reserved for the depressed classes in the general elections.

This was a serious setback for Mahatma Gandhi and the Congress as a whole. Gandhi ji was in Yervada Central Jail, Poona (now Pune), at the time. This news was a thunderbolt for him. Failing to persuade Ambedkar, Gandhi ji went on a fast unto death inside the jail starting 20 September 1932. The whole nation was offering prayers for the long life of their supreme leader.

Madan Mohan Malaviya was a close friend of Ambedkar's, whom the latter held in high esteem. Malaviya persuaded Ambedkar and he yielded. In a meeting in the jail, Gandhi ji reportedly told Ambedkar that he had always cared for the untouchables, even when Ambedkar was not born, and there was no justification for him to accuse Gandhi of being indifferent to the plight of the untouchables. Ambedkar was bold, outspoken and unyielding. He lamented that instead of laying emphasis on khadi, Gandhi should have asked those joining the Congress to

---

[2]Narake, Hari, et al. (eds), *Dr Babasaheb Ambedkar: Writings and Speeches, Vol. 17, Part I,* Dr Ambedkar Foundation, Ministry of Social Justice and Empowerment, Government of India, 2020.

break bread with the untouchables. The arguments continued for some time and at last Ambedkar gave in. Although Ambedkar agreed with Gandhi ji for the moment, there was no real union of hearts. But at last an agreement was reached with the signing of the Poona Pact.

Ambedkar was a voracious reader and a prolific writer. He often visited the Jama Masjid area in search of old books. It is said about him that he would sit through the night, reading one book or the other. It was during this period that he wrote very scathing articles about what was happening within the Congress party. He and his followers kept away from the freedom movement. However, at the same time, they were not with the British. Ambedkar was primarily concerned about the plight of the untouchables. He took out long marches with his followers, holding a mirror to the nation about their sufferings. He was of the opinion that Gandhi only offered platitudes to the British. He could not have been more forthright than when he said, 'Mr. Gandhi is not only not playing the part of a friend of the depressed classes, but he is not even playing the part of an honest foe.'[3]

Ambedkar practised in the High Court of Bombay. He won almost all the cases that he contested. In one of the most famous cases, he defended three non-Brahmin leaders who had accused the Brahmin community of ruining India and were then subsequently sued for libel. His books, *Annihilation of Caste* and *What Congress And Gandhi Have Done To The Untouchables,* presented a rare spectacle of the misery and suffering of the poor and the attitude of the Congress and Gandhi ji about them. Being the most qualified man of his time, his identity was very dear

---

[3]Roy Choudhury, P.C., *Gandhi and His Contemporaries,* Sterling Publishers, 2008.

to him. He stood by his principles like a rock. His intellect and brilliance were unmatched. His legal acumen and his drafting skill were also unparalleled.

Gandhi and the Congress kept up the pressure on the British government through their *satyagraha* (firm adherence to truth) politics. The revolutionaries played a stellar role in creating a sense of panic among the British. In a distant land, Subhas Bose was making a war cry through his Indian National Army. It was a happy coincidence that Winston Churchill, known for his hostility towards India, lost the general elections after the Second World War. A liberal leader, Mr Clement Atlee, came into power and his party decided to grant independence to India. The Indians were asked to draft their Constitution. All eyes, without exception, turned to Ambedkar for the drafting of the Constitution.

In the Constituent Assembly, Ambedkar was unanimously elected as chairman of the drafting committee. He accomplished the job in an inimitable manner with the choicest of words and phrases. The Constitution of India was adopted on 26 November 1949. Ambedkar, who was treated like an eyesore in his earlier days, emerged as the man of the hour. Everyone across party lines showered rich praises on him.

Pandit Nehru invited him to join the Union Cabinet in 1947 as law and justice minister. He continued in this position for a period of almost four years. He resigned on 27 September 1951, as he was not satisfied with Nehru's foreign policy, his attitude to the Kashmir problem and, more importantly, the government's indifference towards backward and scheduled castes. Ambedkar made it clear that power had no meaning without service to the people.

Ambedkar's life was one of struggle. He was fed up with the Hindu ideology of division of society into castes. He had said as early as in 1935, 'I am born a Hindu but [will] not die a Hindu.' He was drawn towards Buddhism and eventually, along with lakhs of his followers, he adopted Buddhism on 14 October 1956. He died on 6 December 1956. His death was mourned throughout the country as a great and tragic loss.

The Government of India recognized his services and conferred on him the highest civilian award, Bharat Ratna, in 1990. A tall statue of Ambedkar was installed in the Indian parliament. Hundreds of institutions, universities and organizations have been named after him. Lakhs of his followers observe his birthday with a rare sense of sanctity and reverence. Political parties observe his birthday more as a ritual and as a tool of political expediency.

It must be said to the credit of Ambedkar that when no one dared even blink before Gandhi and his leadership, he stood tall and firm in his belief that Gandhi had shown no real concern for the depressed classes. It is unfortunate that even today there is scant regard for the policies and principles for which Ambedkar lived and fought all his life. It is unfortunate that instead of paying attention to the concerns he raised during his lifetime, political parties only pay lip service to his memory and mouth platitudes.

But for the reservations provided in the Indian Constitution, due to the efforts of Ambedkar, not much has been done for the untouchables. Even today, they are not allowed access to some of the temples of worship and denied other privileges, in defiance of the highest court of the land. This is unjust to the memory of Ambedkar. In her book, *The Doctor and the Saint*, published in 2017, Arundhati Roy rightly exposes 'some uncomfortable, controversial, and even surprising truths about the political thought and career of India's most famous and most revered figure'.[4] In doing so, she makes the case for why Ambedkar's revolutionary intellectual achievements must be resurrected, not only in India but throughout the world.

Ambedkar will live in the hearts of people for his brilliance, presence of mind, intellect and legal acumen. Generations to come will recall his services for the backward and depressed classes.

---

[4]Roy, Arundhati, *The Doctor and the Saint: The Ambedkar-Gandhi Debate: Caste, Race and Annihilation of Caste*, Penguin Random House India, 2019.

BABA AMTE

A Helping Hand

Honoured as the modern Gandhi of India, Murlidhar Devidas Amte or Baba Amte was born in an affluent Brahmin family in Hinganghat, Maharashtra, on 26 December 1914. His parents—Devidas Amte and Laxmibai Amte—dotingly called him Baba in his childhood and thus he came to be known as Baba Amte. He was very fond of hunting. At 14, he had a gun of his own and went to the nearby forests for hunting. Later, his parents gifted him a sports car cushioned with the skin of a panther.

Baba Amte married Sadhana Amte, a devout and dedicated wife. Though an extremely rich man, he could see callousness and inequality around him. He once remarked, 'There is a certain callousness in families like my family. My family put up strong barriers so as to avoid seeing the misery in the outside world, and I rebelled against it.'[1] This resistance gave birth to a new light in his mind and he became one of the topmost social activists of all time.

His riches did not mean anything to him unless they were a means to human welfare. Two different incidents changed

---

[1]'Baba Amte: The Fearless Humanitarian Who Healed Hearts and Minds', *The CEO Magazine*, https://tinyurl.com/zenbtnbk. Accessed on 7 March 2024.

the course of his life. First, he defended a girl from the lewd remarks of a British officer. When Gandhi ji came to know of it, he called him *abhay sadhak* (a fearless seeker of truth). Second, when he saw a man (Tulsiram) inflicted with leprosy, he was deeply touched and made up his mind to spend the rest of his time rehabilitating patients suffering from leprosy.

At that time, leprosy was considered a social stigma. Persons suffering from this disease were separated from their families and lived in a separate habitation or colony. Baba Amte proved that leprosy was not a contagious disease. He and his wife, Sadhana, lived and ate with the patients suffering from leprosy. He once remarked, 'I took up leprosy work not to help anyone, but to overcome that fear in my life. That it worked out good for others was a by-product. But the fact is I did it to overcome fear.' He and his wife set up three Ashrams in different areas of Maharashtra to help and rehabilitate leprosy patients. The cured patients were taught manufacturing of handicrafts. It was a miracle that they could earn for themselves and become self-reliant.

Baba Amte was a patriot. He was active during the Quit India Movement. It was here that his law degree came to use, as he became the defence lawyer for those arrested during the course of the Movement. He was responsible for the honourable acquittal of many of them. He followed Gandhi ji in letter and spirit. He learnt the art of spinning, worked on the handloom, and put on only khadi clothes. He led a spartan life. He and his wife went to Gandhi ji's ashram in Sevagram and worked like ordinary ashramites. The only mission in their lives now was to devote themselves to social work. They successfully instilled such a spirit in their children, who walked in the footsteps of their father. Doctors by profession, both his sons opened hospitals in remote adivasi areas and treated the poor, the needy, the downtrodden and those belonging to the depressed classes.

Baba Amte's work did not stop after he became the champion of working with leprosy patients. He took up many more causes in the pursuit of social justice. Like Gandhi ji, he also worked as a scavenger. He worked for the removal of poverty and alleviation of the sufferings of others. He worked for wildlife conservation, ecological balance, and even joined Medha Patkar in the Narmada Bachao Andolan.

It has often been seen that most people belonging to rich families lead a luxurious life. But this was not so with Baba Amte. He spent every minute of his life with those who needed him. In doing all this, he never looked for any credit. He once said, 'I don't want to be a great leader; I want to be a man who goes around with a little oilcan and when he sees a breakdown, offers his help. To me, the man who does that is greater than any holy man in saffron-coloured robes. The mechanic with the oilcan: that is my ideal in life.'[2]

Baba Amte lived a long life and passed away with a sense of fortitude on 9 February 2008. During his lifetime, many awards and titles of recognition came his way, though he did not set much store by them. The Government of India conferred on him a great civilian award—Padma Vibhushan—in 1986. He won more than 50 awards, prominent among them being the Dr Ambedkar International Award, the Gandhi Peace Prize, the Ramon Magsaysay Award, the Templeton Prize and the Jamnalal Bajaj Award. He was also honoured with DLitt degrees from various universities. Innumerable schools, colleges and

---

[2]'Remembering Social Activist Baba Amte, the Man Who Defined the Real Purpose of Life', *India Today*, 26 December 2018, https://tinyurl.com/yc7zf4j5. Accessed on 7 March 2024.

social organizations have been established in his honour. However, Baba Amte is much more than these recognitions. He lives on in his work as a social activist. Just as his work as a social reformer is deathless, similarly his name can never fade despite the vagaries of time.

BEGUM SULTAN JAHAN

Unity in Diversity

Begum Sultan Jahan is remembered today as a pioneer in the fields of education, public health and sanitation. She was the only lady chancellor of Aligarh Muslim University (AMU). She earned many laurels and honours in her lifetime. Born on 9 July 1858, she was declared heiress to the throne of Bhopal. She took over as the Begum of Bhopal in 1901.

As a ruler, she saw to it that there was perfect harmony between Hindus and Muslims. She kept away from any political activity. It is true that Bhopal was only a principality under the British rule, but unlike other rulers and chieftains she kept away from pandering to the British rulers. Instead, as a progressive ruler, she kept the interests of the people of Bhopal in mind and did a commendable job in various sectors to improve their living conditions.

During her regime, people of all communities benefitted from the various progressive measures she put in motion. As a social reformer, she did remarkable work in the field of education. She knew the importance of education and set up many schools. She laid particular emphasis on sending girls to school. This was a revolutionary step in her times, as girls were hardly allowed to move out of their houses. She also took interest in framing proper syllabi for the schools. Begum Sultan's priority was to impart training to teachers. Therefore, only qualified persons were engaged in teaching in the schools. She also realized the importance of technical education and made provisions for imparting practical training in various skills, along with other forms of education.

Begum Sultan knew that the plague was wreaking havoc in many parts of the country. Therefore, she arranged for inoculation and vaccination of the young. The Bhopal principality, under her regime, was free from any serious problems of contagious diseases. She laid a lot of emphasis on sanitation and hygiene.

Besides taking interest in these areas, she also gave importance to agriculture. She knew that agriculture was a gamble during the monsoons. If the rains were plenty, the crops would grow. But if there were no timely rains, the crops would be dry and the farmers would be ruined. Therefore, the Begum helped set up irrigational facilities to aid the farmers. Accompanied by her administrative officers, she visited the villages in her regime and listened patiently to the problems of the farmers. To some problems she found instant solutions and gave immediate instructions to the officers. Other problems needed consultations and were discussed in her court. The problems were never brushed under the carpet. As a result, the fields yielded better crops and the revenue increased. The coffers, which were earlier left dry, filled up.

She brought about taxation reforms as well. Keeping the poor people in mind, she kept the taxation rates at a low level. There was no exploitation. Bribery was banned in her state and anyone found indulging in corrupt activities was severely punished. Similarly, she brought reforms in the army, the police, the judiciary and the jails. In her regime, justice prevailed.

The judges were persons with great integrity and provided justice to the people. The police was not allowed to indulge in high-handedness. Policemen were a civilized lot and did not unnecessarily bother the general public.

Begum Sultan never resorted to discrimination between different communities. She treated Muslims and Hindus alike. She appointed Hindus to high administrative posts and took full advantage of the talent of all communities. In her 25-year rule, there was not a single clash between Hindus and Muslims. In this respect, she followed her mother and grandmother and handled situations with politeness and firmness. If she punished the guilty, she also rewarded talented people.

Her interest in education expanded beyond the borders of Bhopal when the Muhammadan Anglo-Oriental College was converted into AMU by an act of legislature. In 1920, she was appointed as the first chancellor of the University. In fact, she held this post till her death in 1930. She provided liberal financial grants to the University on a regular basis. She was invited to address convocations a number of times. It must have been a treat to listen to her scholarly discourses.

Begum Sultan was a well-travelled person. She was invited to attend the coronation ceremony of King George V in London in 1911. She attended the ceremony wearing her traditional veil. In the course of this visit, she travelled to many other countries including France, Germany, Italy, Spain, Egypt, Hungary and Switzerland. She returned home with rich experiences. Her outlook underwent a sea change. Upon her return, she brought about many improvements in the city of Bhopal. Her developmental projects gave Bhopal a cosmopolitan look.

Another notable feature in the Begum as a ruler was that she never wasted any money on royal parties and midnight revelries. To her, each penny was sacred. The revenue of the state was in a public trust, therefore she took care that every penny was spent for the welfare of the princely state of Bhopal.

Begum Sultan was not hungry for power. She ruled for 25 years, and her gift to the state was governance by the people and for the people. It was a model of participatory management—an experiment in democratic governance. She set an example when she decided to abdicate the throne in favour of her son during her lifetime. She died at the age of 72 on 12 May 1930. She was buried with all sacred Muslim rites.

The name of Begum Sultan Jahan will be remembered as one who ruled the princely state of Bhopal and maintained perfect communal harmony. Her great administrative skills kept the princely state content and prosperous.

BHAGAT PURAN SINGH

The Bearded Mother Teresa

Bhagat Puran Singh has no parallel in North India in the field of social work. Born on 4 June 1904 in Rajewal village, Ludhiana, he was the son of Chaudhuri Chibu Mal and Bibi Mehtab Kaur. He was born into a rich family. Unfortunately, they were reduced to poverty after a drought in Punjab in 1913. Chibu Mal died and Mehtab Kaur was left to fend for herself and her child.

Mehtab was a woman of strong determination and wanted to give the best possible education to her child. After receiving primary education in his village school, Bhagat was sent to the town of Khanna in Punjab for matriculation. Mehtab cleaned utensils, washed clothes and did all types of odd jobs in other households to eke out a living for her family and the education of her child.

Ramji Das (Bhagat's name at birth) failed to make his mark in studies and failed in the matriculation examination. Mehtab Kaur had by then shifted to Lahore for a petty job and managed to send ₹10 every month for her son's studies. When this was of no avail, she got him to Lahore and got him admitted to Khalsa High School. But with no interest in regular studies, he spent most of his time in Dyal Singh Library and browsed a number of books. He became a scholar in his own right and could speak with ease on any subject.

It was at this time that he started visiting Gurudwara Dera Sahib in Lahore. With a spiritual bent of mind, he helped the elderly, the sick, and people with health issues or impairments to reach the holy Granth Sahib. He started working in the gurudwara kitchen and cleaned utensils. The head of the gurudwara was so deeply impressed with him that he called him *Puran Singh* (a perfect Sikh). He converted to Sikhism and, as a humble disciple of the gurus, he decided to dedicate his life to the service of humanity. He took a pledge to remain an ascetic and never married.

Sometime in 1923, a four-year-old male child, suffering from leprosy, was left at the main gate of Gurudwara Dera Sahib. The head of the gurudwara called Bhagat and said, 'Look at this child! The cruel parents have left him in this condition with a hope that the "Guru" will take care of him. He has no name but from now onwards he will be called Piara Singh. I leave him under your care. Look after him and give him all help.'[1]

Bhagat folded his hands in obeisance and brought the child inside the gurudwara. At the time of the painful Partition in 1947, Bhagat put Piara Singh on his shoulders and carried him to Amritsar. He landed up in the Khalsa College refugee camp where 25,000 refugees from West Pakistan were being looked after. He became one of the *sewadaar*s (servants of the people).

---

[1]Incident narrated in a personal interview with Jagmohan Singh, who personally interacted with Bhagat Puran Singh.

Bhagat found that there were others in the camp like Piara Singh. He took three to four of them under his care and started living under a banyan tree close to the Golden Temple. He went from door to door and collected donations and looked after children with health issues or impairments. The number of people looked after multiplied, but so did his courage.

Fortunately for him, he came across one Mr Des Raj Bindra, who helped him with money and material and provided some space for the children to live in. Later, when Gopi Chand Bhargava became the chief minister of Punjab, he gave him some land at Tehsilpura, Grand Trunk Road, near Amritsar, where the first proper *pingalwara* was established. Pingalwara is made of two words. *Pingal* refers to a cripple and *wara* means home. Pingalwara thus means home for the crippled. As time rolled by, the number of such children increased considerably. Money also poured in from all sides because the donors believed that every penny was being utilized properly. Facilities were put in place for food, clothing and education of the children. Bibi Inderjit Kaur is now looking after the pingalwara at Amritsar with over 1,000 children with health issues or impairments.

Bhagat was an environmentalist as well. He warned people against pollution, deforestation, soil erosion, ecological imbalance and falling of the groundwater level. He wrote many books and distributed them free of cost. He went from place to place and delivered lectures on the preservation of wildlife. His mother, ever since his childhood, had taught him 'to provide water to the animals, plant trees and water newly planted saplings, offer food to the sparrows, crows and mynahs, pick up thorns from the paths and remove the stones from cart tracks'.[2]

---

[2]Ibid.

This was imprinted on his mind, and he left no stone unturned to do all this and much more.

Bhagat had followed in the footsteps of Bhai Kanhaiya, who knew no caste, religion or creed in the service of humanity. When some Sikh soldiers complained to Guru Gobind Sahib about Bhai Kanhaiya, saying that he was serving water even to the enemy soldiers, the Guru was pleased and encouraged Bhai Kanhaiya to carry on with his humanitarian tasks. This was in the early part of the eighteenth century.

Bhagat, in the course of selfless service, had before his eyes only the creations of God. It did not matter to him which religion or sect the person came from. So was his attitude towards birds and animals.

Bhagat Puran Singh was conferred the Padma Shri by the Government of India in 1979 for his exceptional service to humanity. Khuswant Singh opined:

> Bhagat Puran Singh was no ordinary mortal but undoubtedly the most loved and revered man in the world. I once described him as the bearded Mother Teresa of Punjab. Mother Teresa had the backing of the powerful Roman Catholic Church, the English press and innumerable foundations to give her money. Bhagat Ji had nothing except his single-minded dedication to serve the poor and the needy. And yet he was able to help thousands of lepers, mentally and physically handicapped and the dying. His name will be written in letters of gold in the history of the world.[3]

[3] 'ਭਗਤ ਪੂਰਨ ਸਿੰਘ ਜੀ ਕੌਣ ਸਨ?', *The Khalsa*, https://tinyurl.com/4btv4e4j. Accessed on 12 March 2024.

He was also bestowed with the title of 'Lokratna'. Many other awards came his way but these did not mean anything to him. Service to humanity was the be-all and end-all of his life.

By this time, the Pingalwara Movement had spread far and wide. It was visible in many towns of Punjab. Bhagat Puran Singh had also set up educational institutions where children were provided free education. He became a household name. But the strain of this onerous task led to him getting seriously ill in 1992. He was 88 at that time. He never recovered from his illness and died on 5 August 1992.

BHOGILAL PANDYA

Gandhi of Vagad

Popularly known as the 'Gandhi of Vagad' in Dungarpur district, Rajasthan, Bhogilal Pandya was born on 13 November 1904. His father, Pitamber Pandya, belonged to an upper-class Brahmin family. Bhogilal received his early education in Dungarpur and later went to Ajmer for higher education. Right from his childhood, he played with boys of all castes and religions, ate at their houses and invited them to his own house, notwithstanding objections raised by his mother.

It is to the credit of Bhogilal that he established a school for rural boys and adults at the age of 15. There was no government help for it. Funds came from friends and philanthropists. After this, there was no going back. There was a flurry of activities in the field of education and he opened dozens of colleges for adivasis and other backward and depressed classes. He was fully conscious that lack of education could be a hindrance to a person realizing their full potential.

One can imagine the twinkle in his eyes when he must have seen an adivasi boy dressed in a smart uniform and on his way to school. Similarly, when he found adults studying in a small classroom or even under the shade of a tree learning the alphabet, his joy knew no bounds. Education alone occupied his time. To him, education was the foundation of social reform. Letters of gratitude filled his house. His father now recognized the social service being rendered by his son and felt proud of him.

Rajasthan was then a princely state which imposed many restrictions on Bhogilal's activities. He had established a Vagad Seva Mandir, which was banned by the princely state for no valid reasons. In 1938, he set up the Seva Sangh dedicated to community service in the districts of Dungarpur, Udaipur, Jaipur and Jaisalmer. The area had a big chunk of adivasis and people from the depressed classes. Healthcare programmes were non-existent at that time. Educational activity was negligible. Being a desert area, there was hardly any crop. Irrigational facilities were also not available.

Bhogilal and his friends took up the onerous task of addressing these gaps and, with their dedication and determination, did a commendable job in the areas of education and community service. He kept moving ahead despite the impediments placed in his way by the rulers of the state. His grit and commitment earned him the title of 'Gandhi of Vagad'.

He became active in politics with the advent of the Quit India Movement launched by Mahatma Gandhi on 9 August 1942. Bhogilal established the Praja Mandal in Rajasthan in 1944, which ultimately led to the merger of Rajasthan into the Union of India after Independence.

Bhogilal was actively associated with many organizations in Rajasthan. His popularity was at its zenith. Hence, his claim to a ministerial position could not be ignored. He became the minister of industries in the Rajasthan Cabinet in 1948 and again in 1956. Later, he got another chance at social service when he was appointed as the chairman of the Rajasthan Khadi and Village Industries Board in 1969 by the then Chief Minister Mohan Lal Sukhadia.

Bhogilal continued in this position till 1977. He spread the message about khadi across Rajasthan and set up many small-scale khadi units. He encouraged people to produce not only khadi but also other items like soap, oil and honey. This gave a boost to the khadi industry in the state. Since his dedication was complete, the result of development of the khadi industry was also enormous.

The strain of heavy work eventually led to a decline in the status of his health. He often remained ill but he still issued instructions from his sickbed. A time came when even this ceased and he died on 31 March 1981. In his death, India lost a great social reformer and an activist who spent his life in the service of the depressed classes. Education and its development was not just a fad for him, and he worked tirelessly for it, particularly in the rural areas.

The Government of India recognized his services to the nation and bestowed upon him the third highest civilian award, Padma Bhushan, in April 1976. The Government of Rajasthan renamed the Dungarpur Government College after him and now it is known as the Shree Bhogilal Pandya Government PG College.

People come and go, and some are simply forgotten for lack of any constructive work. But people like Bhogilal Pandya live through their deeds. As a social activist, the name of Bhogilal Pandya will always remain in the ranks of those who dedicated their entire lives towards the welfare of the people.

BILKEES IDREES LATIF

A Life of Harmony

It was the year 1980. Bilkees' husband, Idrees Latif, was the governor of Maharashtra. Bombay (now Mumbai) was caught up in communal frenzy. Accompanied by a friend, a beautiful gracious lady stood at the Bombay Railway Station. She folded her hands in front of a group of people, asking them to maintain peace. I imagine that her words must have been something inspirational, along the lines of, 'We are neither Muslims nor Hindus. We are human beings. Every holy book has taught us to live in harmony like brothers and sisters.' The crowd nodded in reverence and dispersed.

She went unguarded to places where serious communal clashes were taking place. Her life had no meaning for her if her state was going to be torn apart by communal disharmony. Therefore, unmindful of the danger and threat to her life, she walked through the streets and spread messages of kindness, love, compassion and brotherhood. This was the type of personality that Bilkees had.

Bilkees was born in 1930 with a silver spoon in her mouth. There was nothing much that she could not buy with the ample earthly possessions that her parents had. Her father held a high position with the Nizam of Hyderabad in undivided India, and later became the vice chancellor of Osmania University and

Aligarh Muslim University. He was a man of letters and had the reputation of being someone with great academic merit. Her mother was a French lady whose parents owned hotels in Paris. The couple eventually parted ways, but Bilkees received a tremendous amount of love from her stepmother and, of course, from her father. She got the best possible education and grew into a young girl of matchless beauty. She was married to an air force officer who rose up the ranks and became the air chief marshal of the Indian Air Force. After retiring, he had a stint as an ambassador to France, and still later was appointed as the governor of Maharashtra.

Bilkees was a woman of versatile genius. She was highly qualified and took a lot of interest in education. She was a creative painter and took considerable interest in the development of art and culture within the country. A testimony to this is a mural—a rare artwork of 24 by 8 ft—shown at the Japan Aero Exposition in Osaka in 1970. She also served as the chairman of the National Bal Bhavan and Children's Museum. In her time, as many as 107 *bal bhavans* (children's homes) were attached to the National Bal Bhavan.[1] She came forth with many new creative ideas to bring joy and happiness to young children across the country. She added many new items to the children's museum to make it more worthwhile. She wanted everything to be perfect. To this end, she had the full support of her countrymen, and her husband was also very supportive.

Bilkees founded an organization called the Society for Human and Environmental Development. It was through this organization that she carried out her missionary work with great

[1]'The Everlasting Spirit of Begum Bilkees I. Latif', *You and I*, 29 December 2017, https://tinyurl.com/y4hs339x. Accessed on 13 March 2024.

zeal. Her work was not just for children's homes but also for the children in slum areas. Bilkees' most fruitful work was in the largest slum of the world—Dharavi in Bombay. People there lived huddled together in small huts and the colony was largely dirty. There were also instances of children being exploited.

Bilkees made arrangements for the education of the children. She also took measures to put an end to the exploitation of children who worked in hostile circumstances in the apartments of the rich. She opened new schools in the area and provided facilities for sanitation and hygiene. With her dedicated work, Dharavi became a better and safer place to be in. She was cautioned that work in the slums was hazardous to health. However, she cared more for the inhabitants of the slums rather than for herself and the palatial residence of the governor of Maharashtra.

Bilkees was a profound thinker. She was a prolific reader and a writer of note. She published many articles in journals and newspapers, and also authored a few books. One of these was titled *O Dharavi*. This book gives a graphic account of the plight of the people of Dharavi and the steps she undertook to improve their lives. Another book to her credit is *The Fragrance of Forgotten Years*. This book is the story of her own life, a journey from cosmopolitan Paris to the splendid beauty of Hyderabad. She wrote many booklets and gave vent to her feelings—some full of pleasure, others expressing poignancy and pain.

As mentioned previously, Bilkees was born in a wealthy environment. Though she lived a life of grace and splendour, her heart often reached out to the poor. It was this sensitive heart which pulled her into the slum areas of Dharavi and took her to the streets of Bombay to douse the flames of communal violence. She was a bold and fearless person. She was a woman with indomitable courage—the very epitome of love and compassion—and left an indelible mark on those she met and among whom she worked. Her work was recognized by one and all. The Government of India conferred on her the fourth highest civilian award, Padma Shri, in 2009.

Bilkees died peacefully at the age of 86 on 27 October 2017, with her husband by her side in their house in Hyderabad. Bilkees will be remembered by generations as a privileged person whose heart bled for the poor. She worked with the poor and for them, so that they could lead a life of dignity.

BINDESHWAR PATHAK

The Man Who Started Swachh Bharat

Over a telephonic conversation, I told Dr Bindeshwar Pathak that 'in my estimation and in the estimation of many others, you are a pioneering social reformer of contemporary India who has given millions of untouchables a life of dignity and honour'. I requested him for an interview in my office in Noida. After hearing about my physical disability, Dr Pathak not only readily agreed to include his profile in my book, *India's Greatest Reformers,* but also very kindly agreed to meet me in my office on 22 May 2023. It was a privilege and an honour to see him ushered into my office. My sons and I expressed a deep sense of gratitude to him for taking a few minutes out for us from his busy schedule.

Born in 1943, Dr Pathak was 80 when we met. But filled with energy and enthusiasm, he didn't look more than 60 years of age. Progeny of a rich Brahmin family, Dr Pathak was a sensitive child right from the beginning. With an infusion of divinity in him, he seems to think that all persons are born equal. He could not stand the menace of social discrimination.

When he was barely seven, a woman from a lower caste had accidentally brushed against him. His grandmother was furious and made him swallow cow dung and forced him to drink cow urine as a matter of punishment. As a sensitive child, he felt that this discrimination was bad and needed a solution. The idea to end discrimination was further ingrained in him during his college days. He did his bachelor's and master's in sociology from Patna University. By this time, he had read the works of Mahatma Gandhi and B.R. Ambedkar, who were engaged in the onerous task of removing the stigmas that lead to social discrimination and the dehumanizing act of manual scavenging.

Gandhi ji had passed away by that time but Gandhism filtered through every fibre of Dr Pathak's being. He chose manual scavenging as a subject for his PhD dissertation. It was during this time that he visited the houses and colonies of scavengers. He lived with them, ate with them, and even slept in the same place as them. He saw for himself the miserable plight of these depressed classes. After this, he never looked back. He was hungry for a solution. He was not a mere philosopher who would see a thing and forget it. He was a pragmatic sociologist and a scientist who would not rest till he found solutions to the problems, particularly problems like the dehumanizing act of manual scavenging.

At last, he found a solution when he came up with two *sulabh sauchalayas* in Arrah in Bihar. It was a two-pit pour-flush toilet technology, which was very easy to use. In due course of time, the human waste would end up in manure and even in bio energy. With this initial push, Dr Pathak was triumphant and never looked back. He and his volunteers constructed over 1.6 million household toilets across the country. In addition, more than 10,000 'pay and use' toilets were constructed in public places in crowded cities. He is now in popular demand across the world. Sulabh International is a name to reckon with, but Dr Pathak was a restless soul and kept moving on to other things. He seemed to be humming with Robert Frost:

The woods are lovely, dark and deep,
But I have promises to keep,
And miles to go before I sleep,
And miles to go before I sleep.

Dr Pathak had neither power, nor post, nor money. His resolve is his only mainstay. This keeps him going and he traverses a path full of thorns and thistles. In his long march of over 50 years, he visited every nook and corner of the country and put up more than 1.6 million household toilets. He provided a much needed facility by way of 'pay and use' toilets in public places.

In the process, he found gainful employment for thousands of people and helped them elevate their status in the society. Besides, he also established two vocational centres in Rajasthan (at Alwar and Tonk) where people learn to prepare papad and pickles, do facial training, embroidery work and much more. He was lucky to get the support of Prime Minister Narendra Modi, who put in relentless efforts for Swachh Bharat. His Sulabh International partnered not only with the Government of India (GoI) but also with more than 147 companies in providing Sulabh toilets to ensure that India one day becomes free from open defecation. He was made an honorary brand ambassador of the Swachh Rail Mission.

Dr Pathak was invited by many countries to deliver lectures about his Sulabh International Mission. In a way, he became a roving ambassador of hygiene and sanitation across the world. He visited more than 30 countries. It is a matter of singular elation and pride that United Nations (UN) Development

Programme, UNICEF, UN-Habitat, UN Centre for Human Settlements, the GoI, China, Bangladesh, Vietnam, South Africa, etc., all have adopted this technology. His popularity reached its zenith when Mr Bill De Blasio, the former mayor of New York City, declared 14 April as 'Dr Bindeshwar Pathak Day'.[1]

Dr Pathak's area of activity is, and has always been, the welfare of the needy, the poor, the downtrodden, the tribals and the untouchables. He was fully conscious that untouchables have been ill-treated for ages. Their entry was disallowed into places of worship by the upper-caste Brahmins. Accompanied by five Brahmins, a few friends and 100 women from scheduled castes, he once barged into the Nathdwara Temple in Rajasthan. He was persuasive and faced no resistance, but in the process the temple which had remained closed for the scheduled castes for centuries was thrown open for worship by one and all. Many other such acts of courage and conviction go to the credit of Dr Pathak.

Even though Raja Ram Mohan Roy, Ishwar Chandra Vidyasagar and other social reformers had done commendable work in favour of widow remarriage and restoration of dignity and life of honour for the widows, yet the stigma around widow remarriage has persisted even today. Dr Pathak visited Vrindavan and met elderly widows who were leading a forlorn life bereft of any joy. He met them, spoke to them and persuaded them to mingle with other people freely and without any inhibition. The change was miraculous. These widows started taking part in the festival of colours (Holi), the festival of lights (Diwali) and other festivals as well.

---

[1]PTI, 'New York Mayor Declares April 14 as "Bindeshwar Pathak Day"', *The Economic Times*, 16 April 2016, https://tinyurl.com/4yk7tuxe. Accessed on 13 March 2024.

The Sulabh founder is a renaissance man who combines in his multifaceted personality the traits of a social scientist, an engineer, an administrator, a human resource manager, a social entrepreneur and an institution-builder. He is also a philosopher, writer, poet and promoter of art and culture. What is remarkable about him is that he has ingeniously utilized all these talents to enrich and empower the depressed classes and improve community health, hygiene and environmental sanitation. Thus, he has, with fair amount of success, realized the dreams of Gandhi and Ambedkar—to wipe the tears from the eyes of the last man in society.

In quest of a purposeful life, Dr Pathak has received numerous awards, not only in India but across the globe. To count only a few, he was awarded the Padma Bhushan, the third highest civilian award of the GoI, in 1991. He bagged many other prestigious awards like the Stockholm Water Prize by Stockholm International Water Institute; the Lal Bahadur Shastri National Award; the 23rd Nikkei Asia Prize 2018 for 'Culture and Community' in Tokyo, Japan; the Gandhi Peace Prize; the Indira Gandhi Paryavaran Puraskar; and the International Saint Francis Prize for Environment. While giving the last prize to Dr Pathak, his Holiness the Pope John Paul II lauded him saying, 'You are helping the poor.'[2] I agree with what Brutus said about Julius Caesar:

[2]PTI, 'Bindeshwar Pathak: "Toilet Man of India" Who Founded Sulabh and Pioneered Public Sanitation', *The Economic Times*, 15 August 2023, https://tinyurl.com/26v6pc2a. Accessed on 13 March 2024.

His life was gentle; and the elements
So mixed in him, that Nature might stand up
And say to all the world, THIS WAS A MAN!

Such was the man called Dr Bindeshwar Pathak. Let us salute him, take a leaf out of his life, and dedicate our lives to the service of the nation.

Dr Bindeshwar Pathak died of cardiac arrest on 15 August 2023.

DAYA BAI

A Missionary Zeal

The life story of Daya Bai—a Christian woman earlier named Mercy Matthews—is that of a gritty and courageous woman who presents one of the best examples of how a prosperous person should commit themselves to helping and guiding the poor. In her lifetime, she worked for more than six decades in a tribal area in Madhya Pradesh. Incidentally, Madhya Pradesh has one of the largest tribal populations in India. According to the 2011 census of the Government of India, out of a total population of 125.76 crore, 10.4 crore constitute the tribal population. Other states with a major chunk of tribal population are Maharashtra, Odisha (previously Orissa), Gujarat, Rajasthan and Jharkhand. Only 4 per cent of the tribals get into even the low category of government service.[1]

Tribals have a unique culture of their own. They wear their traditional dress, speak a different language and don't mingle easily with other people. They mostly live in forest areas. It is, therefore, difficult even for their well-wishers to go and work

---

[1]'Census Tables', *Office of the Registrar General & Census Commissioner, India, Ministry of Home Affairs, Government of India,* https://tinyurl.com/4xhh9rzt. Accessed on 13 March 2024.

for the amelioration of their lot, provide them social facilities and build hospitals for their healthcare. Daya Bai plunged into such a dark alley and tried to bring a ray of hope and light in their lives. The path was full of thorns and thistles. But she trod that path unmindful of the pain and pricks in her delicate feet. She achieved a fair amount of success and thanked Christ and Gandhi—both of whom she looked upon as the torchbearers of truth and sacrifice.

Born on 22 February 1941 in a prosperous Christian family in Kerala, Mercy Matthews was the eldest child. She received excellent education in a convent school up to matriculation. The spirit of sacrifice was deeply ingrained in her mind. She decided to become a nun. She moved to Hazaribagh (now in Jharkhand) and became a nun in a convent. She worked as a teacher for a year and a half. She then returned to Kerala and did her master's in social work. She also took a degree in law and was one of the highly educated persons in that area. Her only desire was to serve the needy and the downtrodden. She was a true missionary and sacrificed her happy and comfortable life for the mission of her dreams.

Daya Bai was horrified to see the plight of the Bangladeshi refugees and helped them with all her might. She tended to their wounds, sat by their beds for hours on end, and provided solace and kind words. But her real work lay in store in Chhindwara district in Madhya Pradesh. She moved to the tribal areas of Tinsai and Barul. Initially, she found it extremely difficult to mix with the adivasis. Then, she changed her name from Mercy Matthews to Daya Bai, learnt the tribal language and also started dressing like the local people. This allowed her some space to mix with them. But she had to face verbal abuse, humiliation and even physical assaults from the brokers, middlemen and moneylenders who never wanted the tribal population to come out of their poverty.

However, she faced all this with courage and tenacity, even when she had no money to look after herself. She once wrote:

> I began to bridge the gap between the people and myself. It meant taking on a totally different kind of lifestyle. Having had no financial support for several years, I had to struggle to earn my livelihood and also to economise. There were occasions when I could not afford a meal and so managed with a piece of jaggery and water. However, I noticed that I was never in need of anything in particular.[2]

At this time, something like a miracle happened in her life. She got a share from her father's property after his death. With the money, she bought a small piece of land and built a hut to call her own. She kept a few chickens, birds and cattle and looked after them with motherly care. Now, she had become one of the locals. The people could reach out to her for all types of help. In due course, she did three remarkable things. First, she opened a school at Barul. Second, she created a healthcare facility for the tribals. Third, she started organic farming and taught her skill to the local people. She was now a popular figure among them.

Sree Varun, who made a film on her life, said, 'I discovered

---

[2]Williams, Melwyn, 'Daya Bai the Textbook of Mercy! A Life Extraordinaire: Love Sans Borders', *WFY*, 31 October 2022, https://tinyurl.com/yhc6p7b3. Accessed on 12 March 2024.

Daya Bai while pondering what to do next after my first film. All I had in front of me was an insatiable desire to know more about her and a book called "Pachaviral". I rediscovered her through my film Daya Bai.'[3] Daya Bai was named the *Vanitha* Woman of the Year in 2007. She won the Good Samaritan National Award in 2012.

Later, her attention was drawn back to her home state of Kerala, where a large number of peasants had died on account of the use of endosulfan pesticide in Kasaragod district. When she went to Kerala and learnt the ghastly story of the poor peasants, she went on a hunger strike and called upon the government to provide relief to the victims of the deadly disease. She ended her fast only after receiving a written assurance from the Government of Kerala. Such was her determination.

Daya Bai is a woman who willingly gave up her life of luxury. She is a person who has suffered innumerable trials and tribulations, but has never strayed from her path of righteousness. She is an extraordinary Christian missionary who has never worked for conversion of the tribal to Christianity. Her only goal in life is to do beautiful things for human welfare. She is 83 and people in the country wish her a long life, which continues to lighten the dark paths with beauty and joy forever. Lines of a poem by John Keats can aptly apply to her life:

A thing of beauty is joy forever
Its loveliness increases, it will never
Pass into nothingness, but will keep
A bower quiet for us, and a sleep
Full of sweet dreams, and health and quiet breathing.

---

[3]Ibid.

Call her what you will, Mercy Matthews or Daya Bai. As Shakespeare said, 'A rose will smell as sweet by any other name.' Such a rose is Daya Bai.

DAYANAND SARASWATI

The Right Education

Swami Dayanand Saraswati is one of the foremost religious and social reformers of all times. Two incidents were very important in his life. The first relates to Lord Shiva and changed the course of his life. The second incident took a toll on his life and he died of it on 30 October 1883.

Dayanand Saraswati was born on 12 February 1824 to Karshanji Lalji Tiwari and Yashodabai in Kathiawad. His father was a devout worshipper of Lord Shiva, and taught Dayanand to worship him as well. When Dayanand was eight, his *yajnopavita* (sacred thread) ceremony was performed. This marked his formal entry into education.

Like his father, Dayanand also undertook various fasts. During one of those fasts, he stayed awake the entire night, chanting mantras near the statue of Lord Shiva. Suddenly, a mouse came and ran over the statue and even ate away the offerings. At that moment, Dayanand's faith faltered and he thought that if Lord Shiva could not protect himself against a rat, how could he protect his followers. This changed the whole course of his life. This was a milestone which took him away from idol worship. This was later strengthened by his deep study of the Vedas. Thus, the mouse incident was the first incident responsible for his future course of action.

While at home, he was always in a reflective mood. He saw two deaths in his family one after the other. The first to die was his younger sister, followed by his uncle. Like the Buddha, he started questioning the cycle of life and death. It was during those days that his father thought of his marriage. Knowing what was coming and in no mood to marry, he fled his house. He went out on long pilgrimages and to forest retreats. He sat brooding for hours on end. He even went to the Himalayas in search of truth and busied himself with spiritual pursuits. He was away from home for 25 years.

During this time, Dayanand came into contact with, and under the influence of, Virajanand Dandeesha. The yogi informed him that Hinduism had strayed away from its path of rectitude.

Dayanand promised to purify Hinduism through the messages in the Vedas. His promise was not in vain. He became a wandering ascetic and gathered all knowledge, wherever it came from. His belief in the oneness of God was strengthened and he was totally against any kind of idol worship. In the course of his travels, he often debated the religious scriptures with saints and seers. With a smile on his face, he kept moving ahead. At last, he reached Bombay (now Mumbai), where he founded the Arya Samaj on 10 April 1875. The same year, he wrote a book—*Satyarth Prakash*—that became a beacon of light and a guiding force for all those who followed the Vedas. It is as good as the Bible for the Arya Samajists.

Satyarth Prakash speaks about the 10 tenets of Arya Samaj and how one should lead a life based on the truth as enunciated by the Vedas. He wrote and published numerous books including 16 volumes only on the interpretation of the Vedas. He popularized the movement in his lifetime.

Even after he was gone, he found notable followers in the persons of Lala Lajpat Rai, Vinayak Damodar Savarkar, Lala Hardyal, Mahadev Govind Ranade, Swami Shraddhanand, S. Satyamurti, Mahatma Hansraj, Shyamji Krishna Varma and many others. This indicates the wide influence he had, not only on his own generation but also on the generations that followed.

Imagination staggers when one gets to know that more than a thousand Dayanand Anglo Vedic schools, colleges, universities and other organizations cater to the needs of millions of students in the field of education.

Arya Samaj was not only a religious organization. Dayanand was, perhaps, the first Indian to raise the slogan of 'India for Indians'. He advocated simple living and high thinking. Through weekly meetings of the Arya Samaj, he ordained that the alien rulers must quit India. At the same time, he advised people to shirk belief in the caste system and untouchability. He observed that freedom would not come easily unless we bade goodbye to the social evils. In a way, therefore, he was a precursor to Bal Gangadhar Tilak who thundered in a court of law in Bombay in 1908, 'Swaraj is my birthright and I shall have it.'

The second incident, relating to his death, is very strange. The Maharaja of Jodhpur had invited him to his palace to give sermons on the philosophy of Arya Samaj. On reaching the palace, he found Maharaja Jaswant Singh with a girl called Nanhi Jaan. He told the Maharaja to abjure the girl and lead a simple life. The girl in question was cut to the quick and decided to teach the saffron-clothed sadhu a lesson. She connived with Jagannath, the cook of the Maharaja. Jagannath mixed pieces of glass in the milk administered to Dayanand. He felt excruciating pain and developed bleeding sores on his stomach. Medical assistance at Jodhpur and Ajmer was of no help. Dayanand breathed his last on 30 October 1883, which was incidentally the day of Diwali that year, amid chanting of Vedic mantras.

It is worthy of mention that before Dayanand was shifted out of Jodhpur, Jagannath came to him with folded hands and confessed his crime. Dayanand gave him a bag of money and told him to flee before he was caught. Such was the spirit of his forgiveness.

Swami Dayanand Saraswati created an indelible impact during his time. The ages will remember how a man with such erudite scholarship was born in colonized India and lived a life of righteousness and rectitude.

DEVENDRA RAJ MEHTA

Wipe Every Tear

A bureaucrat of impeccable integrity, Devendra Raj (D.R.) Mehta served in the Indian Administrative Service (IAS) for a period of 36 years. During this tenure, from 1961 to 1997, he occupied positions of eminence both in the Government of Rajasthan and the Government of India (GoI). He was known for his sincerity, honesty and incorruptibility. He was alien to ego, vanity and arrogance. He was extremely sensitive to social problems, particularly problems relating to the disadvantaged sections of society.

Devendra Raj Mehta lost his father when he was just five years old, and has a hazy memory of him. After his father's death, he was taken to Jodhpur, where he was brought up under the loving care of his mother, Lad Kanwar, and his uncle. After his early education in a prominent Jodhpur school, he did his graduation and law from a renowned college (affiliated to Rajasthan University) in the same city. Later in his career, he went for studies at the Royal Institute of Public Administration, London, and MIT Sloan School of Management, Cambridge, United States (US). He grew into a precocious, hardworking young boy and cleared his IAS examination and joined the Rajasthan cadre. He married a gracious and ever-supportive woman named Vimla.

In 1969, Mr Mehta was working as the district collector of Jaisalmer—the district which was at that time suffering from the worst kind of drought. He was travelling to oversee the drought operations when he met with a serious accident and broke his right femur. After being rushed to the district hospital and following the due process of treatment and surgery, the doctors came to the conclusion that the injury was serious and the leg might have to be amputated. To hear such a decision must have been horrible for him. Thankfully, after the initial treatment, he was sent to Jaipur for recuperation and a ray of hope was revived as the amputation was not deemed necessary. The recovery took a long period of five months.

While in his sickbed, he mused to himself, 'In case I had lost my leg, the government would have sent me to England or America for limb fitment at its own expense. However, if my driver or a poor pedestrian were to lose his or her limb, where would he have gone?'[1] This thought gripped his mind and he decided that he would surely try to do something for people with health issues or impairments in the coming years. But where would the funds come from? He seemed to be humming along the tune of the British poet, Christine Weatherly, who wrote about an engine going up the hill:

When you travel on the railways,
And the line goes up a hill,
Just listen to the engine,
As it pulls you with a will,

---

[1]Lekshmi Priya S., 'How an Accident Inspired This Ex-IAS Officer to Give Free Artificial Limbs to Lakhs', *The Better India,* 17 April 2019, https://tinyurl.com/3832sfz6. Accessed on 19 March 2024.

Though it goes so very slowly
It sings this little song,
'I THINK I CAN, I THINK I CAN',
And so it goes along.

Devendra Raj Mehta revealed his intentions to his mother and his wife. Both of them were of a charitable disposition and supported his idea. In hours of loneliness, he reflected deep and long. He thought of Mahatma Gandhi, the father of the nation, whose dream was to wipe every tear from every eye. He went through the holy scriptures and found that compassion for others was the best virtue. He read about Lord Mahavira of the sixth century BCE and found him to be an epitome of compassion. He also read about Albert Schweitzer, who was awarded the Nobel Peace Prize for 'reverence for life'.

He then started preparing a blueprint of his scheme for people with health issues or impairments. On 29 March 1975, he founded the Bhagwan Mahaveer Viklang Sahayata Samiti (BMVSS) in Jaipur. The Samiti was registered as per law and was along non-political, non-religious and non-sectarian lines. The primary objective was to provide mobility and dignity to the handicapped. Over a telephonic interview, he communicated to me that the work required moderate efforts to begin with. Only 8 persons were working on it. The organization could rehabilitate 55 persons during the first year of its operations. One can only imagine the amount of satisfaction that D.R. Mehta must have derived after rehabilitating the first person who came to the clinic. After all, his dream had come true.

The rehabilitation centre grew in size and stature as the years rolled by. Year after year, it flourished. People started coming from all parts of India. Devendra Raj Mehta retired from Indian

Civil Services in 1997. Then onwards, he was more passionately involved in rehabilitation using artificial limbs. The rehabilitation centre helps patients with artificial limbs, calipers, wheelchairs, hand-paddled tricycles, crutches and other aids and appliances. Devendra Raj Mehta saw to it that the rehabilitation was a quick affair.

Sometimes, when a patient with an amputated leg was unloaded from a rickshaw, he would be promptly attended to. The patient and the persons accompanying him would be served snacks and refreshments. Arrangements would be made for their stay and food. In a day or two, the patients who had previously arrived at the hospital in tears, would walk out on their own with smiles on their faces.

Jaipur Foot—a brand associated with BMVSS—is now an international organization. While engaged in a brief conversation with me, D.R. Mehta informed, 'Dr Johar, by now our organization has treated more than 2.5 million people across the globe. It is now the largest artificial foot fitment scheme on Earth.' He is not presumptuous about it.

It was astonishing to learn that BMVSS has signed a memorandum of understanding (MoU) with Stanford University, US, and together they have developed special four-bar linkage knee joints for above-knee amputees. Time magazine, in its edition of 23 November 2009, said that it was one of the 50 best inventions of the world for 2009.[2] Besides, BMVSS has also signed an MoU with MIT University, Harvard. It is not just a joint venture, as these organizations also helped BMVSS with funds. The London Business School and IIMs in India have

---

[2]'Jaipur Foot / Jaipur Knee / Jaipur Limb', *WDO*, https://tinyurl.com/yssfnjha. Accessed on 14 March 2024.

written case studies on the famous Jaipur organization.

In our interview, D.R. Mehta proudly said, 'Bhagwan Mahaveer Viklang Sahayta Samiti has held on-the-spot-artificial limb-fitment camps in 41 countries in Asia, Africa and Latin America. The last of these was held in Palestine.' Devendra Raj Mehta was present at this camp in Palestine in June/July 2023. Hats off to a man at 86 moving about and doing yeoman's service. His urge is irresistible. No ordinary human being at this age would travel to Palestine, which is constantly under threat. But D.R. Mehta did it.

During our interview, he remarked, 'Funds is no problem. Money just comes in. Donors are many and growing, once they realize that each penny will be honestly utilized.' The annual budget of the organization is about ₹35 crore. It comes from foreign agencies, the GoI and other liberal donors. With each passing day, D.R. Mehta is becoming younger and more enthusiastic. He is ever-energetic and works from 10.00 a.m. to 8.00 p.m. every day. He is the darling of the organization. It is this organization that keeps him going. One can feel nothing but pride for such a great social reformer of contemporary India.

It is true that the GoI recognized his services and he was conferred with the third highest civilian award, Padma Bhushan, in 2008. He was also honoured with TECH Museum Award for 'Innovation and Its Use for Humanity' in Silicon Valley in November 2007. He was the recipient of the Rajiv Gandhi National Sadbhavana Award in 2012. The award, which carries a citation and a cash award of ₹5 lakh, was given for his outstanding contribution towards promotion of communal harmony, peace and goodwill. Given the title of 'Rajasthan Ratna', he is also a director on the Europe and Asia Board of the US-based MIT Sloan School of Management. The awards are in plenty. Unmindful of these awards, D.R. Mehta is focussed on how to make the organization more efficient and service-oriented.

It is unfortunate and painful that an organization of such a vast magnitude and a social reformer with a rare vision and aptitude like D.R. Mehta are not given due publicity, either in print or electronic media. Devendra Raj Mehta is not hungry for publicity for himself, but he honestly feels that 'if publicity was not confined only to politics, crime and sports, and if space was given to social service in India, many more philanthropists and social reformers will come forward and the poor in India will be served better'.

DURGABAI DESHMUKH

Nari Shakti

Durgabai Deshmukh was a freedom fighter but she is now better known as a social reformer, who remained an activist and worked for women empowerment all her life. She was born in a middle-class family on 15 July 1909, in Rajahmundry (Rajamahendravaram) in Andhra Pradesh. The story of her life is very interesting. She was married to her cousin, Subha Rao, at the age of eight. But she had the seeds of a rebel right from her childhood. When she came of age, she refused to go to her in-laws' place, as she wanted to continue her studies. Her parents had to give in. Similarly, as a student, she protested when the teacher insisted on delivering a lesson in English. She joined a different school and passed her matriculation examination. Later in life, she started Balika Hindi Pathshala in Rajahmundry to promote Hindi education for girls.

Her call to duty came in 1923 when the annual session of the Congress was held in Kakinada, Andhra Pradesh. She was hardly 14 at the time. Along with the session, a stall for Khadi exhibition was also organized. She worked as a volunteer at the gate of the stall and allowed in only persons with a valid ticket. Pandit (Pt) Jawaharlal Nehru also came to visit the stall, but was refused entry by Durgabai. Organizers ran towards her, quickly purchased a ticket for Pt Nehru and then he was allowed to see the exhibition. While others fumed in anger, Pt Nehru patted Durgabai on the back, as she had done her duty properly.

Durgabai was motivated by Mahatma Gandhi's call for Salt Satyagraha. She broke the Salt Law and was arrested. She was arrested again during the Civil Disobedience Movement. It was only after her release from prison that she graduated and also got her master's degree from Andhra University. She later got her degree in law from the University of Madras (now Chennai) in 1942, and started practising in the Madras High Court. She was very successful as a lawyer. She had command over the language and put forth legal arguments with force.

Durgabai's real role started after India attained independence in 1947. Earlier, she had worked in the Constituent Assembly to frame the Indian Constitution in 1946. Since she was a lawyer, she gave many positive suggestions which were approved unanimously by the Assembly. B.R. Ambedkar had a special word of praise for her.

Durgabai was quite concerned about the plight of women, particularly in the rural areas of India. There was no education worth its name. Women were mainly involved in domestic chores in a male-dominated society. There was large-scale exploitation and sexual abuse. Women belonging to the depressed classes suffered even more. At that time, manual scavenging was still a practice and women belonging to lower classes went from house to house to collect excreta. In return, they were only paid a paltry sum of money. She wanted to do something for the women and their education. She wanted them to join the mainstream workforce of India, like it was in other countries in Europe and in the United States. She wanted women to be equal partners with their male counterparts, rather than being slaves forced to wear a veil even within the four walls of the house.

Durgabai failed to win a Lok Sabha seat in the first general elections in 1952 under the new Constitution. But her talent could not be ignored by Pt Nehru. She was appointed as a member of the Planning Commission. As a member, she mustered support for a national policy on social welfare. This ultimately resulted in the establishment of the Central Social Welfare Board in 1953. She was appointed as the first chairperson of the Board. She had many schemes in her mind, but the government could not provide funds for all of them. Therefore, she invited voluntary organizations to come forward and help. Her focus was on education, training and rehabilitation of needy women, children and people with health issues or impairments.

Durgabai visited China in 1953 and studied how the women were being treated there. They were working in offices, and there was more than a satisfactory arrangement for their education. On her return from China, she prepared a report and discussed it with Justice M.C. Chagla and Justice P.B. Gajendragadkar of the Bombay (now Mumbai) High Court, and also with Pt Nehru. As a result of these discussions, several steps were taken for the welfare of women. Though late in the day, the Family Courts Act was enacted on 14 September 1984 for speedy justice in cases involving women.

Durgabai was appointed the chairperson of the National Committee on Women's Education in 1958. After long discussions and close studies, the Committee presented its recommendations in 1959 as follows[1]:

---

[1]Chakma, Debasis, 'Recommendations of National Committee on Women's Education (1958)', 4 July 2023, https://tinyurl.com/yc5b5h97. Accessed on 19

1. Priority should be given to girls' education.
2. A separate department for women should be created in the department of education.
3. A director of education should be appointed in every state to look after girls' education.
4. Co-education should be started in the area of higher education in colleges and universities.
5. University Grants Commission should earmark special funds for women's education.
6. No fees should be charged from female students up to the eighth standard.
7. Optional subjects should be introduced for female students.
8. Training facilities should be liberally provided.
9. Rural areas should be a special focus for girls' education.
10. A good number of reservations for women should be made in various services in the government departments.
11. Arrangements should be made for adult education in the country.

These recommendations were the result of a comprehensive study. Just as Durgabai had written reports during her tenure in the Planning Commission, she produced documents of great value on women's education for the Committee as well. These recommendations were largely accepted.

Durgabai's talent was further utilized when she was sent to Washington, DC, as a member of the Indian delegation to attend the World Food Congress. While at Madras, she was selected as the president of the Blind Relief Association. As president of the

---

February 2024.

Association, she set up a school-hostel and a light-engineering workshop for the blind. This was yet another act of social service.

Durgabai married the finance minister of India, C.D. Deshmukh, in 1953 and together they lived a very happy life. Her services to the nation were recognized. Many institutions were named after her. Andhra University, Visakhapatnam, has named its department of women studies as Dr Durgabai Deshmukh Centre for Women's Studies. The Government of India conferred on her the second highest civilian award, Padma Vibhushan, in 1975 for her services in the field of women's education. She received the Nehru Literacy Award in 1971 for her outstanding contribution in promoting literacy in rural India. She also bagged coveted international awards from organizations like UNESCO.

As a woman, she could feel the pinch, pain and agony of the illiterate women of India. She could defy her parents but every woman could not be like her. She rose in stature only because she received proper education. Therefore, her total attention in life rested on the development of women's education. If women were properly educated, they could add to the workforce of India and the country would develop. This was the mission of her life. She was committed to this mission till she breathed her last on 9 May 1981. She has depicted a graphic picture of her life story in her autobiography, *Chintaman and I*. She also wrote another wonderful book, *The Stone that Speaketh: The History of 59 Years*.

Durgabai Deshmukh will be long remembered as a social reformer whose mission and purpose in life was to promote women's education.

E.V. RAMASWAMI

The Self-Respect Movement

E.V. Ramaswami is popularly known as the father figure of Tamil Nadu. He was born on 17 September 1879 in Erode, Madras (now Chennai). He could go to school only for five years. At the age of 12, he joined his father in his business.

During his early years, Ramaswami could discern the prevailing inequality and social injustice on account of Brahmin domination. He joined the Congress party in 1919 with the hope of contributing not only in the party's struggle for freedom but also towards the removal of inequality and social injustice on account of gender, caste and religion. He even courted arrest in 1921 in the Non-Cooperation Movement. He was arrested again during the Civil Disobedience Movement.

The Congress recognized his services and he was elected as president of the Erode Municipal Committee. But the problem which haunted him right from the beginning had not yet ended. He was convinced that North Indian Aryan culture tried to dominate South India. Brahmins in Tamil Nadu joined the Congress, as they thought that on account of their caste superiority they would be given positions of power and pelf. Ramachandra Guha, in his book *Makers of Modern India,* writes about E.V. Ramaswami, 'Brahmin priests were a particular target of his polemics—they were, he claimed, corrupt and cunning, as well as sexual predators.'[1] A striking incident occurred in Tamil Nadu when the Congress bigshots insisted on serving separate food to Brahmins and non-Brahmins. This hurt Ramaswami greatly.

At this point of time, Ramaswami recalled his visit to Banaras (now Varanasi) in 1904. He had thought that it would be a holy place worthy of worship. But what he found was the opposite. He found dirt and squalor on the streets. Begging was rampant. Half-burnt dead bodies were floating in the Ganga. Brahmin exploitation was in full display. When he tried to satisfy his hunger in an eatery, he was told the place was open only to Brahmins. The discrimination between Brahmins and the lower castes was more than evident.

One instance of protest against this was the Vaikom Satyagraha. People belonging to lower castes were not allowed to use the public paths or enter the place of worship at Vaikom. A movement was launched by T.K. Madhavan, where thousands of his followers joined him. After a grim struggle, a compromise was reached where only a part of the path was allowed. But the entry to the temple was disallowed. Ramaswami experienced many other such absurd things in the Congress party. He then held a frank discussion with Mahatma Gandhi. On account of these differences with Gandhi, he quit the Congress party in 1925.

After he quit the Congress, the Self-Respect Movement became a full-time task for Ramaswami. Later, he even got the Self-Respect Movement Institution registered. He felt that Tamils were superior to the North Indian Brahmins who tried to dominate them. He also felt that the Tamil language was richer than any other language. In fact, he felt it was the mother

[1]Guha, Ramachandra, *Makers of Modern India*, Harvard University Press, 2013.

of Malayalam, Telugu and Kannada languages. It had its own history and culture. The North Indian Brahmins and elite class wanted to destroy this culture. He fought against this assault and called the North Indian Brahmins hypocrites.

In 1937, when C. Rajagopalachari became the chief minister of Madras Presidency, he introduced Hindi in all Tamil schools. Ramaswami took up cudgels against this imposition and owing to this, Hindi language had to be withdrawn from the syllabus of the schools.

Ramaswami, in a way, became a communist in philosophy after his return from his European tour. He first went to Malaya where he was given a rousing reception. Later, he visited Egypt, Greece, Turkey, the then Soviet Union, Germany, England, Spain, France and Portugal. He stayed in the Soviet Union for three months. On his return, he gave up all religious practices and became an atheist.

Ramaswami was also a rationalist and had a scientific temper. It was on this account that he was against child marriage. His contention was that children were married when it was actually time to educate them. He espoused the cause of widow remarriage as well. He said that poor widows were thrown out as waste. He opposed the cruel Brahmin tendencies and wrote in one of his articles, 'In the name of god, religion, and sastras, you have duped us. We were the ruling people. Stop this life of cheating us from this year. Give room for rationalism and humanism. Any opposition not based on rationalism, science, or experience will one day or another, reveal the fraud, selfishness, lies and conspiracies.'[2] In this respect, he followed the principles

---

[2]'Principle and Legacy of Periyar E.V. Ramasamy', *IndiaNetzone,* https://tinyurl.com/4pdhhkc3. Accessed on 12 March 2024.

enunciated by Robert G. Ingersoll, a popular American rationalist thinker and propagandist.

As time rolled by, Ramaswami came to the conclusion that Tamil Nadu deserved to be an independent state, and only then would the imposition of North Indians come to an end. He became the head of the Justice Party in 1939 which was converted to the Dravidar Kazhagam in 1944, and later set up the demand for a Dravida Nadu. He was now nicknamed *Periyar* (the respected soul). He was enormously respected all over Tamil Nadu.

Despite his differences with Gandhi, Ramaswami always held him in high esteem. He was in disagreement with the pro-Brahmin attitude of Gandhi. On Gandhi's assassination, he said:

> With all his good qualities, Gandhi did not bring the people forward from foolish and evil ways. His murderer was an educated man. Therefore nobody can say this is a time of high culture. If you eat poison, you will die. If electricity hits the body, you will die. If you oppose the Brahmin, you will die. Gandhi did not advocate the eradication of Varnasrama Dharma structure, but sees in it a task for the humanisation of society and social change possible within its structure. The consequence of this would be continued high-caste leadership. Gandhi adapted Brahmins to social change without depriving them of their leadership.[3]

Gandhi paid a price for it and was assassinated by a fanatic Brahmin.

It came as a relief for Ramaswami that Dravida Munnetra

---

[3]'Periyar E.V. Ramasamy', *Scholarly Community Encyclopedia*, https://tinyurl.com/2wk5m62w. Accessed on 12 March 2024.

Kazhagam won the elections in 1967 and since then Dravidians have been in control of Tamil Nadu. For Ramaswami, it was a struggle for social justice. It was an unrelenting struggle and he never wavered in his resolve to strengthen the Dravidian culture.

Ramaswami died an atheist on 24 December 1973 in Vellore, Tamil Nadu. The story of him being an atheist is clearly stated on a statue in Tiruchirappalli. The writing on the statue is: 'God does not exist at all. The inventor of God is a fool. The propagator of God is a scoundrel. The worshipper of God is a barbarian.'[4]

Ramaswami, rightly or wrongly, held on to the belief that the malpractices in society have emerged out of the holy scriptures and the so-called 'God'. In any case, Ramaswami will be remembered as a great social reformer who left an indelible imprint on the sands of time. The Government of Tamil Nadu celebrates his birthday as 'Social Justice Day' since 2021. No tribute can be greater than this.

---

[4]Kain, Damni, 'Periyar Attacked the "Sacred", "Private" Space That Sustained the Degradation of Women', *FORWARDPress*, 17 September 2020, https://tinyurl.com/4hdu233h. Accessed on 12 March 2024.

GOPAL GANESH AGARKAR

The Humanist

A staunch votary of humanism and individual liberty, and a classmate of Bal Gangadhar Tilak in Deccan College, Poona (now Pune), Gopal Ganesh Agarkar was born on 14 July 1856. After his postgraduation in 1880, he devoted the rest of his life to social service. Largely influenced by John Stuart Mill, Spencer, Rousseau and Voltaire, he also came to be known as a product of the Renaissance.

In the initial years after his studies, he worked with Bal Gangadhar Tilak. The duo strongly believed that only an educated society could bring about enlightenment. Therefore, with the support of a few friends, they founded the New English School (an established Deccan Society in Poona) and later set up Fergusson College for higher studies. With their continued effort, they set up many more educational institutions where one and all—without distinction of caste, colour or creed—could receive education. Agarkar particularly took various steps to see that women went to schools and colleges.

Tilak and Agarkar were of the opinion that the press was another mode through which enlightenment could be brought about. India was then a slave country, and the alien rulers were cruel and wily. They ruled India with a heavy hand and resorted to all types of cruelty and barbarism. They sought to divide the society along communal lines. Christian missionaries were at work in order to convert people to Christianity. The policy of 'divide and rule' was being practised. To put an end to the British rule, Tilak and Agarkar founded a weekly newspaper called the *Kesari*. The newspaper contained scathing articles against the British rule. While Tilak's priority in his articles was freedom from British bondage, Agarkar chose to write against the prevailing social evils like child marriage and treatment meted out to widows. He made a case for widow remarriage, education for one and all (particularly for women) and against superstition.

This difference in priorities between the two great writers and thinkers caused rifts between them. Agarkar resigned from the *Kesari* and founded his own paper, *Sudharak*, in 1888. It became clear that Tilak had adopted an uncompromising attitude towards the British. Agarkar was prepared to work under the aegis of the British rule, but laid emphasis on the removal of social evils. He was of the opinion that once these social evils disappeared, there would be light and enlightenment. He believed that in such an atmosphere, people would rise in revolt and dismantle the edifice of British imperialism. During this time, Agarkar was even jailed for 101 days in a defamation case filed by Divan Barve of Kolhapur. During this jail period, he translated Shakespeare's *Hamlet* into Marathi. He also smuggled out many articles which were published in different newspapers under a different name.

His crusade against social evils continued unabated after his release from jail. Even though widow remarriage was allowed, the social stigma regarding it still persisted. He had seen the plight of his two widowed aunts. His relentless efforts brought him only partial success. But for him, the quest for a noble cause was more important than its ultimate success. He was alien to ego and arrogance. His role in the field of education can never be undermined. He was appointed as principal of Fergusson College in 1892 and occupied this position till his death on 17 June 1895. He was only 38 then.

It is a fact, with no scope for any conflict, that if Agarkar had lived longer, he would have achieved much more. But severe bouts of asthma snapped his worldly ties at an early age. His life can be compared to a few lines in Ben Johnson's poem 'The Noble Nature':

It is not growing like a tree
In bulk, doth make man better be;
Or standing long an oak, three hundred year,
To fall a log at last, dry, bald, and sere.
A lily of a day
Is fairer far in May,
Although it fall and die that night.

Bal Gangadhar Tilak stands tall in stature as one of the greatest freedom fighters, but the name of Gopal Ganesh Agarkar seems to have been lost to fathomless darkness. However, those who study his life and character in depth will agree that Agarkar was one of the greatest social reformers of his time.

ISHWAR CHANDRA VIDYASAGAR

Ocean of Knowledge

Ishwar Chandra Vidyasagar was one of the leading social reformers of not just Bengal but the entirety of India. A scholar of repute, a symbol of simplicity and an adamant supporter of widow remarriage, he was born on 26 September 1820 in Midnapore district in Bengal. His parents named him Ishwar Chandra. The last part of his name, *Vidyasagar* (ocean of knowledge), was conferred on him by the Sanskrit College in Calcutta (now Kolkata) for his erudite intellect and scholarship. After this, he was more popular as Vidyasagar than as Ishwar Chandra.

He was a precocious student with a prodigious memory. He received his early education in Sanskrit College and mastered the languages of Bengali, Sanskrit, Hindi and English. During those days, he read the holy scriptures with interest and could quote at random from the Dharma Shastras. He graduated from Sanskrit College in 1839. In 1841, he joined Fort William College, Calcutta, as head of the Sanskrit department. But his interest in teaching was far less than in becoming a social reformer who undertakes various tasks to ameliorate the people, particularly women. He followed in the footsteps of Raja Ram Mohan Roy.

Vidyasagar found widows in a miserable plight, especially due to the practice of child marriage. If a girl got married at the age of eight or 10 and lost her husband, the young girl was supposed to live the rest of her life as a widow. She was treated as a social outcast. Her head was shaved clean. She was forced to wear only white clothes and live a life of isolation in a corner of the house. It is true that with the efforts of Raja Ram Mohan Roy, the practice of sati was banned by an act of legislation in 1829. However, the widows continued to live a life of misery.

Vidyasagar took upon himself the task of fighting for widow remarriage. He was opposed not only by the Brahminical society, but even by his own family. However, he remained adamant in his resolve. He quoted from *Naradsmriti* (a Hindu holy scripture), the Bible and the Quran to prove his point that widow remarriage had always been sanctioned. He took up the matter with the government officials of the East India Company (EIC). He produced two volumes of literature only on widow remarriage. These books were an eye-opener for the society. The orthodoxy was deep-rooted and he had to break the shackles. At last, he succeeded when the EIC, with Lord Dalhousie as governor general, adopted a legislation allowing widow remarriage in 1856. It was a moment of joy for Vidyasagar. It is worthy of note that his own son, Narayan Chandra, later married a widow.

Vidyasagar waged a relentless battle against child marriage and polygamy. Vidyasagar was convinced that if India had to make headway, education was necessary. His emphasis was particularly on women's education. He opened many schools and colleges in Midnapore and the adjoining districts to educate girls. While people in Bengal and elsewhere praised him as a yogi clad in a coarse dhoti and a shawl, he was indifferent to any such appreciation.

Vidyasagar is often called the 'father of Bengali prose'. He rationalized and simplified the Bengali alphabets. His book, *Borno Porichoy,* forms a textbook for the learners of Bengali even today. Besides, he wrote many journals and books to espouse his efforts of improving the lot of the common people, particularly the womenfolk.

Vidyasagar spent the last 18 years of his life in Karmatanr (a Santhal tribal area now in Jharkhand). He lived in a simple house where he opened a school for tribal girls during the day and for adults at night. This was the most satisfying period of his life. This was his music, his food and his love. It was here that he passed away on 29 July 1891 at the age of 70. After his death, Rabindranath Tagore said, 'One wonders how God, in the process of producing forty million Bengalis, produced a man!'[1] During his discourses in 1930s and '40s, Mahatma Gandhi often called Vidyasagar a man whom generations will love to emulate.

---

[1]Mortuza, Shamshad, 'A Man in "Forty" Million', *The Daily Star*, 26 September 2019, https://tinyurl.com/5n6bbzh3. Accessed on 12 March 2024.

JAGAN NATH KAUL

The Philanthropist

A chance meeting with Hermann Gmeiner in 1962 in the United States (US) changed the course of life for Jagan Nath Kaul. He was deeply impressed by the philanthropic personality of Gmeiner and took a decision to dedicate his life to the poor and the disadvantaged children, particularly the orphans of India. This was his lifelong mission.

Many lucrative offers came his way after he completed his postgraduate studies in social welfare and childcare. But the idea of childcare in practice was so deeply ingrained in his mind that on his return to India, in 1963, he had only one obsession and that was to establish SOS Children's Village in India. He had emulated the example of selfless service from his Austrian elder.

He was successful in procuring a piece of land in Greenfields, Faridabad, and set up the first SOS Children's Village, a project of his dreams, in 1964. The SOS refers to Societas Socialis, a social club founded by Gmeiner in Austria in 1949, primarily to help the children of army personnel who had lost their lives in the Second World War. Gmeiner was a rich man and invested considerably in the SOS. The organization later changed its nomenclature and became SOS Children's Villages. The idea had greatly appealed to Jagan Nath Kaul, who spent the entire span of his life in the establishment of SOS Children's Villages across India. At the time of his death in 2008, there were 34 such SOS Children's Villages and 75 other centres catering to the needs of more than 15,000 children.

Jagan Nath Kaul was a Kashmiri Pandit. He was born in Rang Teng in Srinagar on 13 October 1924. He was adopted by his maternal uncle at a very young age. After early education in Srinagar, he graduated from Panjab University, Chandigarh. He got his master's degree and a postgraduate diploma in management from the University of Rajasthan. He then shifted to Delhi and took up an assignment as assistant director in the department of social work in the University of Delhi. But he did not stay there for long and proceeded to Ohio University, US, in 1962, to pursue higher studies in social welfare and childcare. It was there, in early 1963, that he met Gmeiner, a father figure in the field of social service. This meeting germinated the idea of social activism in the mind of Jagan Nath Kaul.

As mentioned previously, he returned to India in 1963. The only idea that gripped his mind was how he could help the disadvantaged children in society. After considerable thought, he opened the first SOS Children's Village in Faridabad. He believed that giving a child a home was like expressing belief in life and the fundamental goodness of people. He lived and worked with this belief all his life. The number of students soon grew to be 270.[1] He contacted many friends and admirers, who came forward to help in this noble task. By that time, money was no problem. He got in touch with the state governments and the Government of India and received a good amount of grants.

His passion and commitment received boost with the

---

[1]Gurtu, G.K., 'Remembering Padmashri Jagan Nath Paul', *ikashmir.net*, https://tinyurl.com/2bush722. Accessed on 19 March 2024.

success of his first endeavour. He opened another branch at Varanasi and named it Kheer Bhawani, and it became quite popular. The institution of childcare through SOS Children's Villages underwent a quantum jump. As time rolled by, he established more than 30 centres across the country and was popularly known as Papaji. He was respected all around by the children, their parents, his friends, the local people and also in government circles.

What was the objective of these children's villages? Identification of orphans and children from disadvantaged sections of the society was the first objective. The second was to invite the parents to see for themselves the arrangements made in the Children's Villages. Arrangements were made for free food, clothes, uniform, books and other residential facilities. The appointment of good teachers was a rather difficult task, but it was ably managed. After the children had completed their education, their rehabilitation was arranged. Some of the students coming out of these schools occupied good positions later in life. Jagan Nath Kaul's only satisfaction was that he was doing a sacred duty in a nation where the condition of underprivileged children was in bad shape.

His work was recognized by one and all. To begin with, he was the director of the first institute he established and later became the secretary general of all his institutions. Still later, in 1989, he was elevated to the position of honorary president till 2007.

Many awards were conferred upon him for his selflessness, efficiency and high level of commitment. He won awards both at the national and the international level. At the national level, he was honoured with the Padma Shri in 2000, the Raja Ram Mohan Roy Teachers Award in 1984, the Rajiv Gandhi Manav

Seva Award in 1995, and the Vayoshrestha Award in 2007. At the international level, he was conferred with SOS Ring and Gold Medal of Honour, Austria, and the 2006 Annual Award for Excellence conferred by the Kashmir Overseas Association, Georgia, in community service. It is difficult to count all the awards that he received from time to time.

Jagan Nath Kaul was quite disturbed by the forced displacement of Kashmiri Pandits from the Valley. He helped the cause of Kashmiri Pandits to the best of his ability and strength. He lived a life of total satisfaction and had no regrets. He died in peace on 16 December 2008 in New Delhi.

JANAKI DEVI BAJAJ

No Time to Cry

Janaki Devi Bajaj is considered one of the leading social activists. She hailed from Madhya Pradesh. Born on 7 January 1893 in the house of Sh. Girdharilal Jajodia of Jaora, she was married to Jamnalal Bajaj, one of the topmost industrialists of the time.

Janaki Devi had no formal schooling. When she was six years old, her father arranged for a teacher who gave her some elementary education at home. After marriage, her husband took great pains and educated her. She became an asset to the Bajaj family.

Janaki was a Gandhian socialist. After Mahatma Gandhi's return from South Africa in 1915, her husband and she found a godfather in the person of Gandhi ji and throughout their lives they followed in his footsteps. Although she took part in the freedom movement and even went to jail, her main forte was working in social reconstruction of the society.

Janaki was conscious of her privilege and, when she looked around, she only found poverty, misery and social and economic disparities. She felt that her husband was on the right track and followed him and his way of life. The die was cast. She was determined to give up her luxurious lifestyle and work for the upliftment of millions of women who were underprivileged, particularly the untouchables.

As the years rolled by, Jamnalal offered a huge chunk of land to Gandhi and persuaded him to set up an ashram in Wardha. Gandhi agreed and set up the Gandhi Sevagram close to Wardha. Jamnalal and his wife looked at the austerity of the inhabitants of the ashram. It must have left a deep impact on their minds. Once, when Jamnalal was touring with Gandhi, he supposedly wrote a letter to his wife saying that gold was a symbol of Kali and might 'breed jealousy and a fear of loss'.[1] That was the day she removed all her gold ornaments and took a vow never to wear gold till her last breath.

She donated all her gold jewellery and diamonds for the welfare of the poor and also as funds for the freedom movement. She encouraged many other women around her to follow her example. She successfully persuaded quite a few. She was only 24 at that time. This was a revolutionary step in those days. Gold has always been very precious to women. But Janaki took the lead in giving it away, and many followed. This sacrifice served two purposes. The first was the end of temptation for gold. The second, and more important, was that the gold went on to grease and oil the machinery of the freedom movement.

Prevalence of the purdah system was another social evil. The system made women slaves in their homes, and they were treated as non-entities. Janaki made up her mind to break this system. She took the initiative in her own house. She removed her veil. She also faced and listened to many dissenting voices but never stopped moving ahead. In a gathering of women, she

---

[1]Jankidevi Bajaj Puraskar, 'TBI Blogs: The Story of Jankidevi Bajaj, Who Gave up Gold, Silks & Purdah to Inspire Hundreds of Indian Women', *The Better India*, 3 September 2016, https://tinyurl.com/3yrmfcc9. Accessed on 19 March 2024.

propagated the removal of veil and exclaimed that if they could not free themselves in their homes, how would they free India. She earned huge praise from none other than Subhas Bose, who lauded her for her courage. It is unfortunate that the purdah system still continues in some parts of India.

Janaki was an epitome of simplicity. She tried her best to instil the habit of simplicity in others as well. She believed that weaving and wearing khadi should become an essential component of the life of every Indian. The wily British sent cotton from India to Britain and sold the finished products in India. To fight against this, she started spinning the charkha. She took to wearing khadi clothes. She established many spinning centres and encouraged women, of rich and poor families alike, to make khadi clothes. She rendered financial assistance in an effort to boost the khadi industry. She was greatly successful in her area and Gandhi felt proud of her endeavours.

The worst evil in the social system of India was the practice of untouchability. No less a person than B.R. Ambedkar had suffered indignity and humiliation in his school life on account of this social evil. It is noteworthy that it was Ambedkar who later was the major architect of the Indian Constitution. Gandhi had brought out a weekly paper, *Harijan*, to bring to light the plight of the untouchables, or *harijans* (children of god) as he called them. Even the right to worship was denied to the harijans.

Janaki discussed the matter with her husband. Both of them felt that orthodox Brahminism was a major obstacle in the entry of harijans into temples. Therefore, the couple decided to build their own temple, the Laxmi Narayan Temple, at Wardha and allowed entry to one and all. It was a revolutionary step in that age of orthodoxy. Janaki even hired a Dalit to cook in her kitchen and they ate the food cooked by him.

A disaster came her way when her husband Jamnalal died on 11 February 1942. When she was crying, Gandhi supposedly walked up to her. He patted her back and told her that instead of crying, it was now time to follow the example of her husband, and try and move on. This support was enough for her.

Independence came in August 1947. By this time, her children had been working hard not only for expanding their industrial empire, but also in their philanthropic activities. But she met Vinoba Bhave and worked for the Bhoodan Movement. She walked with him for hundreds of miles through various provinces of India. She derived great satisfaction from this task. Old age did not deter her. In fact, it spurred her to greater activity. She felt a sense of great relief that the poor landless labourers were getting a piece of land, which they could call their own, due to the efforts of Vinoba Bhave. She died in harness on 21 May 1979.

The Government of India conferred on her the second highest civilian award, the Padma Vibhushan, in 1956. Many institutions have been set up in her name not only by Jamnalal Group of Industries but also by other organizations. It is needless to say that Janaki Devi Bajaj played a stellar role in the area of social reconstruction of India and this has immortalized her name. How one wishes that more people like Janaki Devi Bajaj were there to help the disadvantaged sections of society.

JAVAID RAHI

The Tribal Prism

Javaid Rahi, a renowned figure from the Gujjar community in the union territory of Jammu and Kashmir (J&K), is widely recognized as a tribal social activist, a diligent researcher and an eminent writer. He has been a social activist of prominence and has done commendable work for the Gujjar and Bakarwal communities, bringing into limelight the complexities and vicissitudes being faced by them. His writings and research bring the Gujjars and Bakarwals alive, and the people can see through the prism of his literature.

About 10 per cent of India's population is made up of the tribal community. The Northeast is primarily populated by tribals. Besides Odisha (previously Orissa), Chhattisgarh, Jharkhand, Gujarat, Madhya Pradesh and Rajasthan have a sizeable tribal population. On the whole, tribals are facing a crisis of identity, and are a neglected lot. Their forest lands and hilly stretches are being snatched from them on one pretext or the other. Their culture, their values, their traditions and their way of life are being tinkered with in the name of development.

It goes to the credit of Javaid Rahi that in such a scenario, when tribals are facing a crisis of identity, he has successfully focussed on his community and brought to the notice of the authorities the difficulties being faced by them. Javaid's life is one of total commitment. His journey has been both sad and pleasant. It has been sad because the Gujjar community, by and large, is forced to lead a life of misery and deprivation. It is pleasant because he has looked deep into the psyche of the Gujjar community and brought their issues to the fore.

Hellen Keller, an American author and disability rights advocate, once said, 'I cried because I had no shoes, until I met a man who had no feet.' Likewise, Javaid is a born optimist and has given hope to the aspirations of Gujjars and Bakarwals who suffered many difficulties in life. His literature holds a mirror to the miserable plight of this nomadic tribe.

Born on 1 September 1970 in Chandak village of Poonch district located on the line of control near the Indo-Pak border, he was a sharp and brilliant student. After his elementary education at home, he passed his matriculation from Chandak. He joined the University of Jammu for higher studies and completed his master's and then PhD on tribal languages of J&K in 2006. A promising student, Javaid started writing at an early age. He emerged as a vibrant personality and could have taken an easier course. But he chose to walk through a difficult path and wrote about his tribal community and, thus, did two things simultaneously. He provided the public with good literary works and, at the same time, earned a name for himself as a great social reformer. by bringing to the fore the problems of the Gujjar community. It is creditable that he produced, perhaps, the first dictionary containing 70,000 words of Gujari translated into Hindi. He produced an unparalleled encyclopaedia on Himalayan Gujjars, and brought out a collection of more than 300 folk songs.

One can say on authority today that besides being a social reformer, Javaid is a scholar, linguist, writer, poet, translator, broadcaster and social media influencer. He writes regular columns on issues such as the political and socio-economic rights of Gujjars and Bakarwals of J&K, along with the preservation of their culture and language. As an author, he has a dozen books in Urdu, English and Gujari to his credit, including four monolingual and bilingual dictionaries. As an editor, he has so far compiled more than 300 books and journals including dictionaries, text books, anthologies, periodicals, etc., mainly published by prestigious organizations like the J&K Academy of Art, Culture and Languages, Jammu and Kashmir Board of School Education, Gurjar Desh Charitable Trust and the Tribal Research and Cultural Foundation. In a way, he has been instrumental in creating awareness and galvanizing opinion within the general public, the government as well as the Gujjar community.

As a scholar, he has been regularly presenting research papers and making presentations in seminars and conferences on various sociopolitical and cultural issues (or aspects) of Gujjars, Bakarwals and other J&K tribes, in local and outside universities and other academic fora. As a social media person, he has a large fan following from across the world. He has gained this popularity on YouTube, Facebook and Instagram. A known YouTuber, he is the main content creator in Gujari and regularly produces videos on topics like Gujjar origin, history, culture, folklore, socio-economic issues and nomadic way of life. With 6 crore viewers and over 250,000 subscribers, he got the Silver Creator Award from YouTube.

Javaid has made it his life's calling to highlight the systemic wrongs and injustice being meted out to his community by the erstwhile political dispensations in J&K. Be it the matter of ensuring reservations guaranteed to Gujjars and Bakarwals as a scheduled tribe; their forest rights; issues faced in the times of seasonal migrations; implementation of central laws to protect the nomadic way of life; recognition of Gujari language in the 8th Schedule of the Indian Constitution; or the preservation of the rich heritage of Gujjars, Javaid has been taking up all such important issues with the politicians, concerned authorities and officers.

Looking at his contributions, Javaid Rahi was honoured by the Government of J&K in 2022 for his outstanding contribution to the preservation, documentation and dissemination of tribal culture. He also got the state's highest literary award in Gujari in 1999 from the J&K Academy of Art, Culture and Languages, for his research-oriented book *LoK VIRSO*. He also received the National Fellowship Award from the Ministry of Culture, Government of India, in 2000, to undertake research on tribal and nomadic communities of India, with special focus on Gujjars.

Javaid was also the convener/co-coordinator of the Gujari chapter of J&K Board of School Education and prepared a Gujari curriculum for induction of this tribal language in the schools of J&K up to the tenth standard. He is also a member of the curriculum committee of University of Jammu and designed the syllabus for the master's degree courses in Gujari for the University. Further, he has been a part of the curriculum committee of Baba Ghulam Shah Badshah University, Rajouri, Jammu and Kashmir, constituted to prepare the syllabus for the master's degree in Gujari and Pahari.

As an organizer, he has conducted and organized more than a thousand high-profile literary-cum-cultural meets in various areas of the state, including border areas stretching from Teetwal, Tangdhar and Keran in Kupwara; Uri in Baramulla; Khaneter and

Chatral in Poonch; and Budhil in Rajouri. Javaid has attended many national and international seminars where he made presentations related to Gujjar culture.

When one peeps into the spectrum of his life, one tarries and muses, 'Is Dr Rahi more of a literary figure or a social reformer?' In fact, he is a fine combination of both. He reforms *through* literature. His writings reflect his concern for the Gujjars and Bakarwals and gives the reader a clear idea of where his heart lies.

JYOTIRAO PHULE

Light at the End of the Tunnel

Jyotirao Phule is recognized as one of the foremost social reformers of his times. He was born on 11 April 1827. His father, Govindrao Phule, was a *mali* (his profession was growing fruits and vegetables). The family belonged to a lower caste called Shudras. Jyotirao was a precocious child. He was sharp, intelligent and studious. But he was forced to discontinue his studies after primary education due to his caste and financial constraints. However, friends and admirers of Govindrao, particularly a Christian missionary, persuaded him to send his son to the Scottish Mission School for further studies. Jyotirao then showed the stamp of his intelligence and passed the matriculation examination with distinction. In the course of his schooling, he had made many friends across all communities, including Brahmins.

It was the year 1848. Jyotirao Phule was hardly 21. On the invitation of a Brahmin friend, he went to attend the friend's marriage. Just as he was taking part in various festivities, he was reprimanded by someone for attending the wedding in a Brahmin family. He was pushed and abused. His friend was a mere spectator. At that time, the ground seemed to have slipped from under Jyotirao's feet.

On reaching home, he sat in seclusion and brooded over the

unpleasant happening. He observed the social fabric of the day and how the depressed classes were treated. It was a Brahminical society. Shudras were seen and treated in a bad light. At times, they were forced to wear a dark thread round their neck so that they could be recognized. They were not allowed to walk some of the 'special roads' meant only for the upper classes. It was a pity that sometimes a broom was attached to their back for it to sweep the space on which they were walking. A small pouch was attached on the front side of their necks for them to spit into, as they were disallowed to spit on the road lest a Brahmin happened to tread on the spittle of a Shudra. They were living in extremely poor conditions. The struggle was grim. The shackles of the caste system were hard to break. However, it had to be broken. Jyotirao Phule had made up his mind. The die was cast and there was no looking back.

Besides the bane of the rigid caste system, there were other social evils as well. Child marriage was rampant. Widow remarriage was disallowed. Sati, even though banned by an act of legislature in 1829 through the efforts of Raja Ram Mohan Roy, was still practised in certain parts of India, particularly in rural areas. There was no education worth its name for children of scheduled castes and scheduled tribes. There was no education at all for the girls. The Brahmins ruled the roost.

Jyotirao Phule emerged out of the dark tunnel and launched a scathing attack on the study of the Vedas, the Puranas and other holy scriptures. He was conscious that it was the Aryans who were responsible for the spread of the Hindu culture which divided the society along caste lines.

His father ostracized him. Jyotirao moved away with his wife, Savitribai Phule, four years younger to him, and they lived in a separate habitation. Poona (now Pune) and villages around it soon found their saviour in Jyotirao. They flocked to him in large numbers. He preached to them that it was the holy scriptures of the Hindus which divided them. In due course of time, he had a good following. The Christian missionaries were sympathetic to his cause.

Jyoitrao and Savitribai thought that education alone could bring about enlightenment. Both of them, along with their friends, opened three schools to begin with. The number of students multiplied gradually. Savitribai travelled from village to village to persuade parents to enrol their daughters in the schools. The attempt was successful, and many girls joined the school. Dozens of schools came into being between 1848 and 1857. But when the Revolt of 1857 took place against the government of the East India Company, the schools stopped receiving government funding. However, this did not stop Jyotirao and his wife. They raised funds from friends and supporters, and continued to oil and grease the educational machinery of the schools.

As described earlier, child marriage was in practice. Some girls became widows at a very young age. At times, these widows were also pregnant. The choice before them was three-fold. They could either kill themselves, kill the baby at birth or keep the baby and face the indignities inflicted upon them by the society. Jyotirao and his wife opened an infanticide prevention centre and invited the widows to live with them there. It was promised that their stay would be kept a secret. Many such widows came to live with them, and they provided loving care to the widows.

Savitribai was a strong and visible support to her husband. She taught in one school or the other. Every day, on the way, she was stoned and abused, and mud and cow dung were thrown at her. But she faced everything boldly and went to teach. She had two sarees; she wore one on her way to school, which would often get spoilt with cow dung thrown by miscreants. She changed into the second saree on reaching the school and taught the children. On her way back, she would wear the same spoilt saree.

When the plague or some other disease struck the people in large numbers, they opened many hospitals and took proper care of the patients. They arranged for their food and clothing, and provided all types of nursing. In due course, they became very popular. Jyotirao was given the honorific title of 'Mahatma' in a special function held in his honour on 11 May 1888. He was by then a name to reckon with.

On the strength of charity and his own business of vegetables and flowers, Jyotirao was now a landlord and owned 60 acres of land. He was elected as the municipal commissioner of Poona Municipal Committee. He was a well-known contractor and earned a lot of money. But he knew that the money was worth its name only when it was spent helping the poor, the downtrodden, the Dalits and the needy.

Jyotirao, whom Dr B.R. Ambedkar recognized as his 'master', soon saw a decline in his health. The strain of his work for education, hospitals and other charitable institutions was too much for him. Savitribai and he had no child of their own. They set an example by adopting the child of a widow. The child's name was Yashwant Singh who, later in life, became a doctor. Mahatma Phule passed away on 28 November 1890, leaving behind a glorious example of social service. Many educational institutions, including universities, were established in his name. A postal stamp was issued in his honour in 1977.

But social recognition apart, Jyotirao set a new political discourse. He chalked out a new path where Dalits recognized their own identity and learnt to lead an honourable life in a caste-stricken society. His work is timeless in the annals of social reform. His message is universal and knows no boundaries. Hence, he will always be remembered as a beacon of light for all times to come.

K. VISWANATHAN

Beyond the Walls of a Classroom

A messiah for the socially marginalized sections of society, K. Viswanathan was born on 8 February 1928 in Vellanadu, some distance away from Thiruvananthapuram or Trivandrum (the capital of Kerala). He was bestowed with the rare qualities of head and heart right from his childhood. He received his early education in Trivandrum and went for higher education at Visva-Bharti University in Bengal (now West Bengal). Visva-Bharti is located close to Calcutta (now Kolkata) and was started by Rabindranath Tagore in 1921. He returned home with a degree in *shiksha bhavana.*

His desire to study further took him to the United States (US), then to United Kingdom and still later to Scandinavia. While in the US, he came in contact with Arthur E. Morgan, a great scholar and educator. Viswanathan was deeply influenced by the way Arthur was working, particularly in the field of education. In Denmark, he visited a folk high school, which cast a spell on him because of how cultural values were given importance and how the poor also had a right to education.

On his return to India, he could have easily got into the lucrative profession of teaching or in any other government service. But the influence of foreign scholars on him did not allow his conscience to merely earn money with his qualifications. In addition, he had the influence of Mahatma Gandhi and Rabindranath Tagore writ large on his personality. He decided to serve the rural people in India.

He went to his village home in Vellanadu and, on a 60-acre tract of land, he founded Mitraniketan, which became a centre for learning through practical training. He established various units like residential schools for tribal children, Mitraniketan People's College, *Krishi Vigyan Kendra* (Farm Science Centre), Rural Technology Centre, training and production centres, bakery, fruit processing centre, and pottery and coconut fibre activities. Mitraniketan attracted a good number of students, mostly from rural areas, who worked part-time while learning in Mitraniketan. It was built on the pattern of Tolstoy Farm started by Gandhi in South Africa, where people from all walks of life were given training in the development of various skills.

Mitraniketan was earning fame far and wide on the strength of its products. It attracted many foreigners for purposes of research and they later showered rich encomiums on Mitraniketan. K. Viswanathan was not working for any profit. He was a rich man in his own right. He derived happiness and satisfaction when he saw so many people working and educating themselves at his centre. According to him, the main areas of focus of Mitraniketan were education; the development of sustainable agriculture and rural technology; and the empowerment of women. He started getting invitations from within India and abroad to aid and advice the opening of such centres at different places. He chaired many national and international conferences. He worked on various advisory boards of government and non-government institutions.

Even though he was an important figure, he led a simple life on Gandhian principles. He lived for the sake of others. The main focus of Viswanathan was to develop rural areas through technology. Many organizations across the country and abroad recognized his distinctive services. He was conferred with the Padma Shri by the Government of India in 2009. As early as in 1992, he was honoured with the Jamnalal Bajaj Award for application of science and technology in rural areas. He was also honoured with the Henry Dunant Red Cross Award, and was given the Platinum Jubilee Endowment Trust Award by Indian Merchants Chamber in 1986. Awards came in aplenty. It is difficult to count them. It is also not important to name them all in this brief essay.

In any case, he never ran after awards. He was above them all. His only satisfaction was that he was imparting training to students of rural India. He was helping the poorer sections of society. His wife, Sethulaxmi, was very supportive in all his actions. However, the strain of work told on his heart. He suffered from heart-related problems and passed away on 28 April 2014 with the full knowledge and belief that he had done a pious duty given to him by God. His main principle of life was enunciated by him in these words:

> Education does not circumscribe learning within the walls of a class or the pages of a book. Education is also about equipping youngsters with life skills and vocational training. A sense of purpose motivates employees and volunteers because they are aware that their work can make a difference to improve living conditions of the underprivileged in society.[1]

---

[1]Nagarajan, Saraswathy, 'School of Thought', *The Hindu*, 11 September 2013, https://tinyurl.com/5n68zcyn. Accessed on 12 March 2024.

KAILASH SATYARTHI

Saving Children and Their Childhood

A social reformer par excellence, Nobel Peace Laureate Kailash Satyarthi is one of the leaders and the loudest voice speaking for the oppressed and voiceless. Satyarthi has been threatened numerous times for his relentless efforts in combating untouchability, caste system and other social evils such as child labour and child marriage. Despite the risks, he has personally rescued thousands of children from the scourge of slavery and has become a powerful voice for the marginalized. His dedication to these causes is unparalleled, and he has made an immense impact on the lives of those he has helped. His fearless and unrelenting policy advocacy efforts towards elimination of violence against the powerless has resulted in path-breaking legislations globally.

From expelling the caste system and all the beliefs that lead to untouchability, Kailash Sharma gave up his family surname to become Kailash *Satyarthi* (a person in search of the truth). He became a student looking for the deeper meanings of life. It certainly wasn't an easy journey for a 15-year-old boy, to take such a decision and abide by it till date.

Compassionate to the core, he led Dalits and untouchables inside the Nathdwara Temple and put an end to the oppression that had been going on for years. The whole nation lauded this move and the former president of India, R. Venkataraman, expressed his desire to visit the Nathdwara Temple with Dalits and untouchables.

Satyarthi left a lucrative career as an electrical engineer and started the *Bachpan Bachao Andolan* (Save Childhood Movement) to rescue children from the shackles of slavery, paving the way for their reintegration into mainstream society with the help of state actors under the legal policy framework of India.

Renowned for pushing for inclusion of child exploitation in the global sociopolitical agenda in 1998, the Nobel Laureate conceived and led one of the largest civil society movements—the Global March against Child Labour—traversing 103 countries covering 80,000 km, with a demand for an international law against worst forms of child labour. This eventually led to the adoption of the ILO (International Labour Organization) Convention No. 182 on worst forms of child labour. This was formally acclaimed in 1999, and went on to become the fastest ratified convention in the history of the ILO.

He then went on to successfully spearhead a countrywide movement to make education a constitutional provision, which subsequently paved the way for the right of children to free and compulsory education in 2009.

Satyarthi's contribution in the fight against social evils for close to four decades has been acknowledged internationally. Several prestigious awards have been conferred on him, including the Defenders of Democracy Award in 2009 in the United States (US); Alfonso Comin International Award in 2008 in Spain; the Medal of the Italian Senate in 2007; Robert F. Kennedy International Human Rights Award; Aachener Friedenspreis (Aachen Peace Prize) in Germany; and the Fredric Ebert International Human Rights Award, also in Germany.

As one of the rare civil society leaders, Satyarthi has addressed the United Nations (UN) General Assembly, International Labour Conference, UN Human Rights Commission, UNESCO and several parliamentary hearings and committees in the US, Germany, the United Kingdom, Italy, Brazil, Panama, Nepal, Spain and Chile, to name a few.

A global thought leader, Satyarthi has been at the forefront of demanding social protection for vulnerable children living in African nations and other low-income countries. For him, every minute matters, every child matters and every childhood matters.

In the wake of the brutal gang rape and murder of a 23-year-old paramedic student in Delhi in December 2012, Satyarthi played a pivotal role in steering Indian civil society towards a demand for amendments in the Indian Criminal Law to counter rape and gender-based violence. This eventually led to the promulgation of Criminal Law (Amendment) Act, 2013.

In 2014, he was awarded the Nobel Peace Prize for the 'struggle against the suppression of children and young people and for the right of all children to education'.[1]

Satyarthi's sustained efforts to end child slavery, trafficking, forced labour and violence received international support when he succeeded in getting child protection and welfare-related clauses included in the sustainable development goals of the UN back in September 2015.

Satyarthi envisions a world where the youth realizes its truest potential as the agent of positive social transformation. Almost 70 now, his compassion for all things living has him going as strong as ever, and he will not stop till all the voiceless find a voice.

---

[1]'Press Release', *The Nobel Prize*, https://tinyurl.com/55k2fbbn. Accessed on 12 March 2024.

KANDUKURI VEERESALINGAM

The Right to Remarry

Popularly known as the 'Raja Ram Mohan Roy of Andhra Pradesh', Kandukuri Veeresalingam attained an eminent position as a social reformer. His courage and daring to do what he thought was right had no match. He rose from poverty and deprivation to achieve a position as a man worthy of emulation in society. In a way, he brought about a Renaissance resurgence in Andhra Pradesh. Born on 16 April 1848 in Rajamahendravaram (Rajahmundry) village in Andhra Pradesh, he lost his father when he was only four. He was brought up by his paternal uncle with great care. At the age of five, he was admitted into a government primary school. He showed signs of growing into a promising youth and learnt many stories from the holy scriptures of ancient India. In his high school, he was declared as one of the best students and passed his matriculation in 1869. He had a brief stint as a teacher and later rose to be the headmaster of Rajahmundry School.

As he grew older, Veeresalingam came face to face with the backwardness of Andhra Pradesh. He had read the life stories of Raja Ram Mohan Roy, Ishwar Chandra Vidyasagar and Keshab Chandra Sen—all from Bengal. He was deeply impressed by their ideas and made up his mind to put them into practice. He became increasingly conscious that nothing could be achieved without education. Women were the most neglected lot in this area. Therefore, in association with a few friends, he opened a school for girls. Later, he opened a co-educational school as well. The plight of the girl child was miserable. Just when it was the age for her studies, she would be married off. In *Viveka Vardhini* (his weekly paper) and *Satithitabodhin* (a monthly magazine), he laid a lot of emphasis on women's education.

Veeresalingam was against child marriage. He also vehemently espoused the cause of widow remarriage. He greatly appreciated Raja Ram Mohan Roy and Ishwar Chandra Vidyasagar for their contribution towards the abolition of sati and supporting the cause of widow remarriage, respectively. He became a staunch follower of Brahmo Samaj. He also castigated those who favoured the *devadasi* practice.

If a girl became a widow, she was pushed into the corner of a house and treated like an inauspicious creature. She was forced to shave her head, wear white clothes and was not allowed to mix with any other member of the family. Veeresalingam thought this to be a silly practice and pleaded the case of widow remarriage. He was opposed, intimidated and physically assaulted by the upper-caste Brahmins. Undeterred, he made a move against the prevalent social order. He silenced his critics by quoting verses from the holy Hindu scriptures that supported his argument. His joy knew no bounds when he arranged the marriage of a widow in 1881. In his lifetime, he arranged the marriages of 40 more widows. Nothing gave him more pleasure than rehabilitation of the widows.

Veeresalingam fought against the superstitions prevailing in society. He made efforts to widen the range of knowledge in society and to modernize Andhra Pradesh. There was an incident where he was asked for bribe money to get a government service.

He refused to bribe the officer and rather remained out of a government job. Later, he wrote against the officials saying that they were mostly corrupt and dishonest.

Veeresalingam was a prolific writer. Apart from his two journals, he was the first novelist of Andhra Pradesh. His first novel, *Rajasekhara Charitramu,* became quite popular. Reading about the trials and tribulations of Rajashekhra of the fourth century awakened the conscience of the people of Andhra Pradesh. He was the first author to write his autobiography in Telugu, and was also the first to write the history of Telugu poets. He also translated a large number of science books into Telugu to help the students. This effort of Veeresalingam was greatly appreciated.

The British government was so pleased with him that they bestowed upon him the title of 'Rao Bahadur'. This was done to honour his modern outlook and his efforts to raise the people from the deep slumber of superstitions. His wife also supported him in his endeavours. Veeresalingam died on 27 May 1919 with the satisfaction of having devoted his life to social reforms which went a long way in modernizing Andhra Pradesh. As a mark of respect to him, a statue of him was made on Beach Road in Visakhapatnam. The Government of India issued a 25-paisa postage stamp in his honour in 1974. Yet, it is not these honours, but his actions of service to society that has immortalized him for eternity.

LOTIKA SARKAR

The Crusader

Lotika Sarkar, an eminent lawyer, shot into fame when she (along with a few other advocates) wrote an open letter to the Supreme Court of India which had acquitted two policemen in a rape case that took place at Mathura. The acquittal was on the basis of consent. But Lotika Sarkar and others argued the following, 'Consent involves submission, but the converse is not necessarily true... From the facts of case, all that is established is submission, and not consent... Is the taboo against pre-marital sex so strong as to provide a license to Indian police to rape young girls?'[1] The rape case against the policemen was reopened and the earlier judgment of the Hon'ble Supreme Court of India was revoked.

Lotika came from an aristocratic family in West Bengal. She completed her graduation from the University of Cambridge, United Kingdom. Later, she completed her PhD from the University of Cambridge in 1951. Immediately after the completion of her degree, she joined the faculty of law at the University of Delhi (Delhi University or DU). There were only

---

[1]'Case Brief of Mathura Rape Case of 26th March 1972 by Shrutika', *TogetherWCWW*, 7 July 2021, https://tinyurl.com/2jd69cyc. Accessed on 12 March 2024.

10 girls in the class. But as time passed, the number increased to 80 in the 1960s. As if her thirst for knowledge in law was not enough, she went to study international law at Harvard University in the United States. After this, she was second to none in the interpretation of constitutional law but her main focus remained on the rape cases taking place across India.

If Lotika was alive today, she would be flabbergasted to see the number of rape cases happening every day in India. The young and the old alike rape girls and mostly get away with it. The Nirbhaya rape case shook the conscience of the nation, and Delhi was more or less shut down for a few days. There were large-scale demonstrations leading to closure of shops. After this, new laws were adopted. The judgments came more expeditiously and conviction rate increased considerably. Even POCSO (Protection of Children from Sexual Offences) came into being and the arrest of the accused after an FIR was lodged was made immediate. But, even today, the influential find ways to escape the police, mostly by exerting political pressure.

While still in the DU faculty of law as the head of the department (and later as dean), Lotika was associated with two important associations, namely the Centre for Women's Development Studies (1980) and Indian Association for Women Studies (1982). Dr Vina Mazumdar, along with Lotika, did everything possible for the education of women. Wherever there was social injustice and cruelty against women, these associations became active and found solutions. It was with their efforts that women's education across the country picked up pace and a large number of girls came out and joined the universities. This revolution in education, particularly in law, goes to the credit of Lotika.

Lotika married Chanchal Sarkar in 1957. Her husband was a man of great intellect who started as assistant editor of *The Statesman* and later became the founding director of the Press Institute of India. He was also a great help to the efforts being put in by Lotika in fighting for the rights of women. He died in 2005 but Lotika remained vigilant and continued her crusade against cruelty and injustice towards women.

It can only be called an irony of fate that she found herself in a legal tangle when her tenant disposed of her house in an illegal manner. The legal fraternity came to her rescue and she ultimately won the case. It is very strange that such a case can happen even to a famous lawyer who worked all her life to get justice for others.

After retirement from the law faculty of DU, she taught criminal law at the Indian Law Institute for more than 10 years. Lotika Sarkar's service-oriented attitude in the legal profession will always be remembered with respect.

MADAN MOHAN MALAVIYA

The Karmayogi

Pandit (Pt) Madan ohan Malaviya was not only a great freedom fighter but also a prominent social reformer. During the freedom movement, he suffered imprisonment a number of times and was thoroughly Gandhian in approach. He was the only man who was elected as Congress president four times—in 1909, 1918, 1932 and 1933. He even accompanied Mahatma Gandhi for the First Round Table Conference in England in 1931. He criticized the British government through his scathing articles published in various newspapers like *The Opinion, Leader, Hindustan Times* and a few others. Gandhi ji was so deeply influenced by Malaviya that he called him *Mahamana* (the great soul). Dr S. Radhakrishnan, who later became the president of India, gave him the title of *Karmayogi.*

When Gandhi ji returned from South Africa in 1915, Pt Madan Mohan Malaviya impacted his political course. Gandhi ji said:

> I found him (Tilak) as Himalaya, I thought that it was not possible for me to climb that an unscalabel (sic) height. I then went to Shri Gokhale. He appeared to me like a deep ocean. I found that it was not possible for me to enter so

> deep. Lastly, I approached Malaviyaji. He seemed to be as crystal like as the stream and I decided to have ablutions in the sacred stream.[1]

This was a great tribute to Pt Madan Mohan Malaviya.

Malaviya was born into a Kayastha family on 25 December 1861 in Madhya Pradesh. His father, Brijlal, though scholarly, was a poor man. After receiving his early education in the Malwa region of Madhya Pradesh, he later shifted to Banaras (now Varanasi). He would not write either Kayastha or Srivastava as a subcaste. Since he had been born in the Malwa region, he came to be known as Madan Mohan Malaviya. This amply proves that he was not a casteist. He was not a pandit by caste either. He came to be known as Pt Madan Mohan Malaviya on the strength of his learning and scholarship. Throughout his life, he tried to unite people who were divided along caste lines.

He went to Calcutta (now Kolkata) for his graduation on a scholarship given by Harrison College's principal. He got a degree in law from the University of Allahabad and started his legal practice in 1893. He saw roaring success in his practice, but he gave it up in 1911. Two thoughts led him to this decision. First was his desire to break free from the British yoke of slavery. The second was his will to disseminate education in India.

He was of the opinion that if Indians continued to be illiterate, they would not feel the pinch of slavery. They would never know what a free nation was. Therefore, he approached his lawyer friends like Pt Motilal Nehru, Sh. Tej Bahadar Sapru, Purushottam Das Tandon and many others and raised

---

[1]Pandey, Vishwanath, *Pandit Madan Mohan Malviya and the Formative Years of Indian Nationalism*, LG Publishers Distributors, 2015.

funds. He set up many educational schools. Further, he was of the opinion that education for girls was equally important. Therefore, he established a few schools for girls.

His quest for higher education took him to Annie Besant. She had founded the Central Hindu College in Banaras in 1898. Together, they thought of opening a university. His efforts bore fruit in 1916 when Banaras Hindu University (BHU) was established. Today, BHU is one of the largest universities in the world. The University is particularly known for its research component. Pandit Malaviya remained the vice chancellor of this University from 1919 to 1938. After 1938, Dr Sarvepalli Radhakrishnan became its vice chancellor. Thus, for more than anything else, Malaviya's name will be counted among the founders of higher education in India.

Malaviya was a devout Hindu. However, he was stoutly against the practice of untouchability. For him, members belonging to the depressed classes were as good a creation of God as a Brahmin. He led the movement to ensure the entry of scheduled castes and give them the right to worship at many places, particularly the Kalaram Temple in Nasik. He castigated the so-called upper castes and told them that the worship of God was an inherent right of every person.

Malaviya was disturbed by the Communal Award brought in by the British government in 1932. This was a clever ruse on the part of the alien rulers to divide India along caste lines and to alienate the scheduled castes from the upper-caste Hindus. Gandhi ji undertook a fast unto death as a mark of protest against it. Dr B.R. Ambedkar was at last brought to agreement by Malaviya and, as a result, the Poona Pact was signed on 24 September 1932. This is how Gandhi ji's life was saved.

Malaviya was against the system of bonded labour being practised by the British and the rich landlords of India. He wrote against this practice in various newspapers and brought about an awakening. He led many movements against this slavish practice and freed a large number of people who were considered slaves by the rich and the influential.

Malaviya always stood for Hindu–Muslim unity. He had many Muslim friends and they worked together to achieve this end. They knew and clearly understood that the British policy of divide and rule was malicious in nature. The Partition of Bengal in 1905 was one such instance. The British rulers had to withdraw the order of the partition in 1911 in the face of stiff resistance. Malaviya was of the view that unless the Hindus, Muslims and people of other religions put up a joint fight against the British, they would not leave India.

As mentioned earlier, Malaviya had given up his legal practice in 1911. But he wore the legal robes once again in the wake of the Chauri Chaura incident in Bihar in 1922, in which 22 policemen were burnt alive by an angry mob. As many as 170 persons were ordered to be hanged to death. Malaviya thought this to be an act of grave injustice. He contested the case in a court and was successful in securing acquittal orders for as many as 155 prisoners. The remaining 15 also escaped the gallows and were sentenced for life. He did this to fight against the wrong being done by the British rulers.

Malaviya continued to take interest in the advancement of education and the elimination of the caste system from Indian society till his last breath. He died on 12 November 1946, when India was only 10 months away from freedom. After India achieved freedom, his services were recognized by the grateful nation. Many places were named after him, and educational institutions were set up in his honour as well. A tall statue of Malaviya stands in the Indian parliament. It was on 24 December 2014 that he was conferred with the highest civilian award, Bharat Ratna, for his services in the field of education and his role in the freedom movement.

MANASI PRADHAN

Work is Dharma

Manasi Pradhan is a brave reformer from Odisha (previously Orissa). She rose to the present eminent position owing to her desire to help the society from a young age. She was born on 4 October 1962 in Ayatapur in Khordha District, Odisha. It was a very backward area with no schools around. She received her primary education in her village. But her father was a poor farmer and was in no position to send her for any further education. Then there was also a safety concern, as the only high school in the area was 15 km away. But Manasi was possessed with an irresistible desire to receive higher education. Therefore, she used all her persuasive skills with her parents and joined the Patitapaban High School. She travelled 15 km back and forth every day.

Manasi did not stop here. After her matriculation examination, her interest in higher education intensified. Her father could ill-afford it. All the same, the family moved to Puri where she joined the Government Women's College. It was here that a tragedy overtook the family, and her mother died of cancer. It was an unbearable agony for her and her family. Her father was bedridden, and the entire burden of her two younger siblings (a brother and a sister) fell upon her shoulders. But she carried on, took up some work and bore the expenses of the family. After graduation, she did her master's in Odia literature from Utkal University, Bhubaneswar. She also got a law degree from G.M. Law College, Puri.

A braveheart, she did a stint in the finance department (Government of Odisha) and also in the Andhra Bank. And that's not all. She was made of even sterner stuff and became an entrepreneur. She set up a printing press with her savings, and with the help of friends and admirers she successfully brought out the *Josodhara* magazine. The magazine became popular and she reaped considerable financial benefit from it. But all the while, her heart was yearning for something bigger and better. Her heart was yearning not for profit, but for social service.

Right from her childhood, she had seen the miserable plight of the girl child and women in society. She wanted to do something to improve the condition of women and bring them out of this slavish position. With this in mind, she founded Odisa Yuva Sanskrutik Sansad (OYSS) Women.

The initial objective was to educate the young girls in order to prepare them as future leaders. She held many workshops in different parts of Odisha and spoke to women about their rights. She told them about the miserable situation of the women in the country, particularly in Odisha. She also organized camps to prepare women for self-defence in case they have to deal with domestic violence.

It is shocking to note that Indian society, even after 75 years of Independence, continues to fight against social injustice, largely based on gender bias. According to official data, 31,677 cases of rape and 6,589 cases of dowry deaths were reported across India in 2021 alone.[1] But this, perhaps, is the tip of the

---

[1]'Nearly 20% Increase in Rapes across India in 2021, Rajasthan Had Highest Cases:

iceberg. The figures may be much higher in each category. It was this social injustice that Manasi had been fighting against all her life.

Manasi founded the Honour for Women National Campaign. The primary objective of this movement was to end violence against women in India. It galvanized the workforce of women in different parts of the country to put an end to atrocities against them. The misfortune, however, is that when violence against women takes place in urban areas it comes to light immediately, in view of an active electronic and print media; the same does not happen in the rural areas. Moreover, it has been noticed that these atrocities and domestic violence usually take place on account of consumption of liquor.

After considerable consultation with women's help groups and organizations all over the country, Manasi came up with a four-point charter of demands and sent the same to all state governments and the Government of India for necessary action and implementation. These four points were:

1. complete clampdown on liquor trade;
2. self-defence training for women as part of the educational curriculum;
3. special protection force for women's security in every district; and
4. fast-track courts and special investigating and prosecuting wing for crime against women in every district.[2]

NCRB', *The Wire*, 30 August 2022, https://tinyurl.com/f68ydwb2. Accessed on 12 March 2024.

[2]Sharma, Anjali, 'Manasi Pradhan: Champion of Women's Rights and a Beacon

This was in 2014. In the same year, she launched Nirbhaya Vahini to mobilize public opinion and engaged in a sustained campaign against domestic violence. This could be controlled through the implementation of the four-point charter created by her.

Manasi is a versatile genius. Besides writing scathing articles that speak about violence and atrocities of all kinds against women, she produced a book, *Urmi-O-Uchchwas,* of a tall order. The book, written in Odia, has since been translated into eight languages across the country. She wrote some poignant poems giving a graphic account of the miserable plight of women.

A great social reformer and a great women's rights activist, Manasi never sought any reward for her work. While speaking to an interviewer, she said, 'I don't have some goal of being a rich woman; if I'm getting food, and I have a roof over my head, that's more than enough.' She further added, 'For me, my work is my God, and the faith to do work is my dharma.'[3]

In the course of her painful and happy journey, she won many awards and accolades. One might say that the above statement is a paradox. How can the journey be both painful and happy? It was painful on account of her striking poverty, and happy because she overcame all her difficulties and worked for women in such a glorious manner. She was conferred with the Rani Lakshmibai Stree Shakti Puraskar in 2014 by the then president of India, Pranab Mukherjee. She was one of the recipients of the Outstanding Women Award in 2011. New York-based *Bustle,* a magazine, termed her as one of the

---

of Empowerment', *The CEO Magazine,* https://tinyurl.com/3yspzkhp. Accessed on 19 March 2024.

[3]'Interviewing Manasi Pradhan', *YP,* April 2017, https://tinyurl.com/57m3hsye. Accessed on 19 March 2024.

20 most inspiring feminist authors and activists. On the other hand, Los Angeles-based Welker Media Inc. counted her as one of the 12 most powerful feminist change-makers. She has won many more awards. It is difficult to count them all.

Manasi Pradhan, an outstanding woman activist, was invited to address the Oxford Union (of the University of Oxford). She has the credit of serving on the Inquiry Committee of the National Commission for Women and on the Censor Board of India. A woman like Manasi Pradhan will always find an honourable place in the history of social activists.

MARTHA FARRELL

The Martyr

Martha Farrell was born on 5 June 1959 in Delhi, amid jubilation in her family. Her death, however, came far from home. She was assassinated (along with 14 others) on 13 May 2015 at a guesthouse in Kabul by terrorists, in one of the most gruesome and barbaric attacks. At that time, she was holding a gender training workshop in Kabul. It was well known then, as it is now, that the Taliban in Afghanistan suppressed the women in all walks of life. Nine years have rolled by since her death. The condition of women in Afghanistan has worsened; girls are not allowed to go to school and thus remain illiterate. The civil society in Afghanistan cannot even think of gender equality.

Afghanistan is only one example. Gender inequality prevails in most countries of the world, with the exception of a few developed countries. Mahatma Gandhi, Savitribai Phule, Jyotirao Phule and many other social reformers in India have done their best to stir the conscience of mankind to consider women as equal partners. They have met with only partial success. The goal is still far off. It's a mirage, difficult to achieve.

Yet, constant efforts have been made by people who have worked on gender equality and women's education. Martha Farrell was one such woman having grit and determination.

She had done her postgraduation in social work in 1981 from the University of Delhi and PhD from Jamia Millia Islamia in 2013. During her postgraduation, she observed that only a few women came forward for higher education. The dropout rate at the lower levels was disastrous. She believed that a society in which only a small number of women were receiving education could never dream of gender equality.

After 1981, she had a brief tenure in teaching, but soon went into social work. She focussed her attention on three areas:

1. Bringing gender equality
2. Women's education
3. Speaking up against sexual harassment at workplaces

The percentage of women going to schools and colleges was precariously low. This led to gender inequality. Even otherwise, women were kept under a veil for generations on end. They were engaged only in domestic chores. But lately, when there has been improvement in women's education and they have shown their worth and capabilities in different fields, they are found to be vulnerable to sexual harassment at workplaces. Efforts have been made for their safety. But cases of sexual harassment appear in electronic and print media on a daily basis. This is utterly disgraceful. Parents, therefore, fight shy of sending their daughters to workplaces where safety is not ensured. This is the case particularly when women work in night shifts.

This condition of women wounded Martha Farrell's heart. Then, her total attention was on working for the safety of women in their workplaces. One of her friends, Nandita Bhatt, said about her:

> When I heard everyone talking about Martha being a perfect mother, sister, daughter, daughter-in-law, wife and a perfect woman—I knew she would have been screaming! I think she was the perfect human being. I carried her casket from the ambulance to the conference hall and carried her out of it—amidst the protests of our 'typically' male colleagues. She would have been screaming at them then too, I know! I am proud that I could do that for her—and for all that she stood for.[1]

Martha Farrell worked day and night in Participatory Research in Asia (PRIA) founded by her husband, Rajesh Tandon, in 1996. In this regard, she worked in Delhi and went to different places across the country and abroad, and delivered lectures on sexual harassment in workplaces. As the director of PRIA's programme on gender mainstreaming in institutions, she worked among thousands of women in urban and rural areas and imparted training to them about gender equality, local governance and sexual harassment. Her training programmes were attended by many and appreciated.

It's a pity that Martha Farrell died young, at the age of 55. Had she lived longer, she would have achieved much more. It is regrettable that the then Government of India or even the Delhi government did not take notice of women like Martha Farrell, who lived and died for the crucial cause of gender equality and saving women from sexual harassment in their workplaces. However, there were a few who recognized her services and set

---

[1]Sengupta, Isha, 'Martha Farrell: The "Everyday Feminist" | #IndianWomeninHistory', *Feminism in India,* 7 March 2019, https://tinyurl.com/3uhs3ddx. Accessed on 12 March 2024.

up the Martha Farrell Memorial Fellowship and Martha Farrell Award for Excellence in Women Empowerment. This award is given every year. One of the awardees, Rakhi Gope, observed, 'I will tell all the girls in my community of this feminist, Martha Farrell, and through her life inspire them to become feminists.'[2]

Martha Farrell, in her lifetime, came to be popularly known as an 'Everyday Feminist'. It simply means that she was engaged in uplifting women, and providing education and assuring safety to them at all times. This seemed to be the sole purpose of her existence. She lived for it and died for it. In fact, she died a martyr to this cause.

---

[2]Ibid.

MARY CLUBWALA JADHAV

Care and Share

A woman with an insatiable thirst for social service, Mary Clubwala Jadhav was one of the greatest philanthropists of her times. She was a charming and gracious person. She was born in a hilly tract of Ootacamund (Ooty) in Tamil Nadu on 10 June 1908. She did not go to any educational institution. Her father, Rustom Patel, was a rich, Parsi businessman and arranged for her education at home. At times, she could be seen practising for her Trinity College piano exams on a mild summer afternoon in 1918, in the sylvan surroundings of the Nilgiris. Thus, her upbringing was very luxurious and she could enjoy every comfort at home.

Mary was married to Nyogi Phurey Clubwala in 1926 and led a happy married life. They had a son named Khusro. Soon after her marriage she realized that India was basically divided into two parts, the rich and the poor. The poor lived a life of privation and could hardly afford two meals a day. At times, they slept hungry. She was drawn to social service and doled out money to various charitable organizations. She was actually acting on the advice of her mother, who had taught her a lesson for life when she gave her the sermon of 'caring and sharing'. Now, Mary wanted to care for everybody and share the grievances of the poor. She had identified her lot in the needy, the downtrodden and the disadvantaged sections of society.

While she was having this rich experience, a tragedy struck in her personal life and she lost her husband. He had gone to Europe for treatment where he lost his life in 1935. She felt lonely and desolate but remained brave at heart. She refused to give in and moved ahead. It is at this critical juncture that she joined the Guild of Service, which was started by Mrs Waller in 1923. She worked very hard and was appointed the honorary secretary of this organization.

The Guild did various activities and set up various projects like health centres, bakery units, an adoption centre, family-assistance schemes, meals on wheels, rural development projects, a school for the deaf, and many more. The organization kept itself free from the stigma of gender and caste bias. It also gave particular attention to the untouchables. It went ahead and looked after leprosy patients and those suffering from tuberculosis as well. They were served with nutritious food, and the results were very encouraging.

In 1942, the Madras (now Chennai) Presidency had an influx of soldiers wounded in the Second World War. They had very scanty pay and hardly any people to look after them. Mary established an Indian Hospitality Committee. It looked after the soldiers with great care and sympathy. It organized mobile canteens, hospital visits, diversional therapy and entertainment programmes. After the War was over, this Committee was renamed as Prisoners' Welfare & Ex-servicemen's Welfare. The Committee served so well that it attracted the attention of one and all. General Cariappa called Mary the 'darling of the Army'.

Mary was the first woman to set up a school for social work in 1952 under the banner of Guild of Service. It was one of the two social work schools, the other being the Tata Institute of Social Sciences. Her school ran courses in community development, medical and psychiatric social work, human resource development, international studies, etc. Mary had taken care that the school was second to none. She had visited the United States and studied the functioning of various social work schools before setting up her own. That explained the tremendous success of the school.

Mary remarried in 1953. Her husband, Chandrakant K. Jadhav, was from the Army and was a very committed social worker. He helped his wife in the advancement of her various charitable initiatives. It is worthy of note that in the late 1930s, Mary was appointed as the juvenile court magistrate, an office she held for 15 long years. She was also appointed as the honorary presidency magistrate. This was a rare honour for Mary. It was her capacity for work that helped her keep busy with the courts and simultaneously look after the Guild of Service. In 1956, she became the first woman sheriff of the Madras Presidency.

Mary had, by then, become a household name in Madras. She was conferred with the Padma Shri in 1955. This motivated her to work harder. By then, she was engaged with 150 organizations throughout the country. She was also conferred with the Padma Bhushan in 1968. She was honoured with the Outstanding Service Award by the International Council of Social Welfare at Hague in 1972. She was conferred with the second highest civilian award, Padma Vibhushan, in 1975. It was a matter of great honour for Mary that the first president of India, Dr Rajendra Prasad, and many governors acted as honorary presidents of the Guild of Service.

Mary, the shining star, passed away on 6 February 1975. But her glory can never fade away. The phenomenal work done by her all her life can never be forgotten. She will always be recognized as a person dedicated to the service of humanity. Remembering her, Himani Datar, honorary secretary of the Guild of Service, paid tribute and said:

> The guild still forges ahead with her vision for service. We have more than 20 welfare projects and 10,000 people under our care at the moment, from training institutes for special educators, to another for handicapped children, day care centres for the aged, financial and nutritional support for children with leukemia, and counselling services at women's prison in Puzhal. We are a volunteer-run organisation, so right now, the real need is more volunteers. The organisation is almost reaching its centenary year, and we need more hands on deck to keep the wrong going.[1]

Women like Mary Clubwala Jadhav are only born once in centuries.

---

[1]Maithai, Kamini, 'Book on "Poster Girl of Social Work" Mary Clubwala Jadhav to Be Penned', *The Times of India*, 11 June 2017, https://tinyurl.com/y3wevk5p. Accessed on 12 March 2024.

MAHATMA GANDHI

The Father of the Nation

Mohandas Karamchand Gandhi, popularly known as Bapu or Gandhi ji, was born on 2 October 1869 at Porbandar, a coastal town in Kathiawad, Gujarat. Although not a Nobel laureate himself, he influenced Nobel laureates like Nelson Mandela and Martin Luther King, Jr. He is a man for all times and all seasons. Volumes have been written on him and many more can still be written on his multifaceted personality. But the scope of the present essay is limited only to his work in the area of social reform.

His work in social reform can be divided into two parts: the work done in South Africa between 1893 and 1914, and in India from 1915 till his tragic death. In South Africa, he fought a relentless battle against the white colonialists who discriminated against people of colour. His personal experience had also been bitter, even though he was a barrister. He was stopped from boarding the first-class compartment in a train, even though he held a valid ticket. He was often beaten and thrashed but he never lost his cool. Rather, he gathered around him thousands of South Africans and other migrants to wage a peaceful satyagraha against the colonialists.

He was jailed a number of times in South Africa but his resolve to continue with the struggle was only strengthened. His devoted wife, Kasturba, joined him in the struggle and later looked after the Tolstoy Farm set up by him in Johannesburg. This was the farm where people (mostly of Indian origin) were taught the skills of carpentry, metal working, welding, agriculture, shoemaking, etc. Gandhi ji himself learnt the art of shoemaking. Before his departure for India in 1914, he stitched a pair of sandals and sent it to General Smuts. The latter sent the sandals back to Gandhi ji on his seventieth birthday saying, 'I have worn these sandals for many a summer...even though I may feel that I am not worthy to stand in the shoes of so great a man. It was my fate to be the antagonist of a man for whom even then I had the highest respect.'[1] So deep was the understanding between General Smuts and Gandhi ji, even though Smuts had jailed Gandhi ji a number of times during his struggle against apartheid in South Africa.

Gandhi ji sailed back to India on 19 July 1914 at the invitation of Gopal Krishna Gokhale. On his return, he met the three great men of India at that time: Bal Gangadhar Tilak, Gopal Krishna Gokhale and Madan Mohan Malaviya. Gandhi ji later said:

> I found him (Tilak) as Himalaya, I thought that it was not possible for me to climb that an unscalabel (sic) height. I then went to Shri Gokhale. He appeared to me like a deep ocean. I found that it was not possible for me to enter so deep. Lastly, I approached Malaviyaji. He seemed to be as crystal like as the stream and I decided to have ablutions in the sacred stream.[2]

---

[1]Singh, Rahul, 'Gandhi's Chappals & Smuts' Sandals', *The Tribune*, 2 October 2019, https://tinyurl.com/3vv8ahnr. Accessed on 12 March 2024.

[2]Pandey, Vishwanath, *Pandit Madan Mohan Malviya and the Formative Years of Indian Nationalism*, LG Publishers Distributors, 2015.

There is no denying the fact that Gandhi ji, with the support of his followers and other freedom fighters, attained freedom for India with his weapons of truth and non-violence. But his work in the social field cannot be undermined. For him, all men and women were equal. He was against the practice of untouchability. For Gandhi ji, these people were *harijans* (children of God). In fact, he started a weekly paper, *Harijan*, from 11 February 1933. This was an effort to put an end to the evil practice of untouchability. When the British rulers tried to create separate constituencies for the depressed classes, Gandhi ji opposed it tooth and nail and went on a fast unto death. At last, the problem was resolved by the signing of the Poona Pact on 24 September 1932.

Gandhi ji firmly believed that empowerment of women was of utmost importance. Women, who had hitherto remained aloof and were confined to domestic chores, came out and received education, and started playing a role in the social order. Gandhi ji advised one and all to lead a simple and truthful life. He popularized charkha-spinning and people started wearing khadi clothes.

Gandhi ji worked with rare zeal to bring about religious and ethnic amity. He was against all kinds of fanaticism and tried his best to bring about Hindu–Muslim unity. But it is an irony of fate that Gandhi ji died at the hands of a fanatic while coming out of a prayer meeting in Birla Temple, New Delhi. It happened on 30 January 1948. The whole country was plunged into grief. In a condolence telegram to Pt Nehru, Albert Einstein said, 'Generations to come will scarce believe that such a one as this ever lived in flesh and blood walked upon this earth.'[3]

---

[3]PTI, 'PM Moots "Einstein Challenge" in Tribute to Mahatma Gandhi in NYT Op-Ed', *The Economic Times*, 2 October 2019, https://tinyurl.com/66c3k3rh. Accessed on 12 March 2024.

Thus ended the luminous career of someone who had struggled all his life for the Indian freedom movement and for the removal of social evils from the face of society. Pt Nehru, while announcing Gandhi ji's death in the Indian parliament, said, 'The light has gone out of our lives.'

It is a great tribute to his personality that he is called the 'father of the nation'. Every head of state from abroad goes to Gandhi ji's samadhi to pay their respects, when on an official visit to India. Many memorials have been raised in his name, both in the country and abroad. Generations to come will remember the tall and slim man, clothed in khadi, for his accomplishments in life. India has never produced, and is not likely to produce, a man of the stature of Mahatma Gandhi, who fought the mighty British imperialism with truth and non-violence.

MOTHER TERESA

The Saint

Mother Teresa became the symbol of service in Calcutta (now Kolkata) after she founded the Missionaries of Charity. After a humble beginning with just 13 nuns, the Missionaries of Charity now has its branches in various countries of the world, with thousands of nuns who have taken a pledge of chastity and obedience in the cause of helping the needy. Mahatma Gandhi had once said that the mission of his life was to wipe every tear from every eye. Mother Teresa and her clan took a similar stand to help 'the hungry, the naked, the homeless, the crippled, the blind, the lepers, all those people who feel unwanted, unloved, uncared for throughout society, people that have become a burden to the society and are shunned by everyone.'[1]

Mother Teresa took her first religious vow on 24 May 1931. She was born as Anjezë Gonxhe Bojaxhiu on 26 August 1910 in Macedonia. She was only eight when her father died. Her mother raised her to be a beautiful, intelligent girl of great merit. When she was 18, she was determined to engage herself in helping

---

[1]'Mother Teresa Was an Embodiment of Compassion: President Mukherjee', *Business Standard*, 3 September 2016, https://tinyurl.com/4v5263nj. Accessed on 19 March 2024.

the suffering humanity. She left home and went to the Sisters of Loreto at Loreto Abbey in Rathfarnham, Ireland, to learn English with the intent of becoming a missionary. After she had learnt English, she left for India in 1929. She spent a year in Darjeeling, where she worked as a teacher at St Teresa School.

Later, she went to Calcutta and joined Loreto Convent School and worked there for a few years, first as a teacher and then as its headmistress. She took a solemn pledge on 14 May 1937 to care for all like a mother would, following the Loreto custom. She was at Loreto Convent School for almost 20 years.

But there was a restlessness in her soul; she was not satisfied with what she was doing. She felt an inner call to go into a wider sphere of work. She must have felt as if Jesus told her to abandon teaching and go to the slums of Calcutta, aiding the city's poorest and sickest people. She resigned as headmistress in 1946 and was determined to help the destitute.

In 1950, she received the Vatican's approval for setting up Missionaries of Charity within the premises of the Roman Catholic Church in Calcutta. It was a modest beginning. But the number of nuns under the banner of Missionaries of Charity grew as time rolled by. She set up as many as 19 centres in Calcutta alone. There was a separate centre for lepers, a separate one for the elderly, another for the sick, and so on. Her popularity grew. In the meantime, she received some basic medical training and nursed the sick with her own hands. Wearing a white saree with a blue border, she moved from one centre to the other and guided the nuns in those centres. Unmindful of the initial financial constraints, she spent all that she had earned over the years. A time came when donations came pouring in large numbers, enabling her to render better service to humanity.

By now, Mother Teresa had become an international icon in the field of social service. She was invited by many countries, where she helped set up centres under the banner of Missionaries of Charity of Calcutta. She was by then serving millions of people across the world. Her services were recognized by the Government of India (GoI), which conferred upon her the highest civilian award, the Bharat Ratna, in 1980. Earlier, she had received the Nobel Peace Prize in 1979. While conferring the award, the Norwegian Nobel Committee said in their motivation, 'In making the award the Norwegian Nobel Committee has expressed its recognition of Mother Teresa's work in bringing help to suffering humanity. This year the world has turned its attention to the plight of children and refugees, and these are precisely the categories for whom Mother Teresa has for many years worked so selflessly.'[2] While receiving the award, Mother Teresa said that abortion was the greatest destroyer of peace. She received a lot of criticism for this statement. To quote her:

> We are talking of peace. These are things that break peace, but I feel the greatest destroyer of peace today is abortion, because it is a direct war, a direct killing—direct murder by the mother herself. And we read in the Scripture, for God says very clearly: Even if a mother could forget her child—I will not forget you—I have carved you in the palm of my hand. We are carved in the palm of His hand, so close to Him that unborn child has been carved in the hand of God.[3]

---

[2]'The Nobel Peace Prize 1979', *The Nobel Prize*, https://tinyurl.com/3hx7cdbw. Accessed on 19 March 2024.

[3]'Mother Teresa: Nobel Lecture', *The Nobel Prize*, https://tinyurl.com/mwknfkc2. Accessed on 12 March 2024.

Mother Teresa touched the zenith of popularity when she received the United States' highest civilian award, the Presidential Medal of Freedom, in 1985. She won more than 120 prizes and recognitions from all over the world. But unmindful of the awards, she continued her work with greater zeal and enthusiasm.

Amid this glory, Mother Teresa was denounced on three major counts. She was charged with financial bungling and misutilization of funds. Even an author, Robert Fox, criticized her saying that her doctors only occasionally visited the patients and that the pain relief provided to the dying was inadequate, leading them to suffer unnecessarily. Secondly, she was alleged to have converted the patients to Christianity. But when Mother Teresa was asked about this charge, she replied, 'Yes, I convert. I convert you to be a better Hindu, or a better Muslim, or a better Protestant, or a better Catholic, or a better Parsee, or a better Sikh, or a better Buddhist. And after you have found God, it is for you to do what God wants you to do.'[4]

As mentioned earlier, she was also criticized when she spoke against contraception. She was of the view that it was for God to give life and to take away as well. It was so ordained and human beings should not interfere with it. The GoI, then working to check the rising population in the country, was critical of her statement. But Mother Teresa stood steady on her track. Notwithstanding these critical remarks, she continued to get immense popularity with each passing day.

A noble soul, she bade adieu to her mortal frame on 5 September 1997 in Calcutta. She was given a State funeral

---

[4]Fisher, Simcha, 'Why Didn't Mother Teresa Push for Conversions?', *Aleteia*, 9 June 2016, https://tinyurl.com/5bhmsvyb. Accessed on 12 March 2024.

by the GoI in gratitude for her service to the poor of all religions from across the country. Cardinal Secretary of State, Angelo Sodano, the Pope's representative, delivered the homily at the service. It was a great tribute indeed. She was canonized by Pope Francis, the highest Roman Catholic authority, on 4 September 2016. Mother Teresa is now a revered saint in the prayers of all those who adhere to Roman Catholic religious ideology. She is immortal and her service is eternal.

NARAYAN SINGH MANAKLAO

The Complete Reformer

Narayan Singh Manaklao has attained international recognition as a social reformer for his work in the areas of de-addiction from opium, care for polio, aged care and environmental protection. A man imbued with enthusiasm, he plunged himself into social service. He left his lucrative job as professor at Magadh University and focussed on helping the suffering people in Rajasthan.

Therefore, he returned to his village—Manaklao, Jodhpur. Some parts of Rajasthan faced the problem of opium consumption. He saw this in his own village where most of the people were addicted to opium. He was a well-known person in his village. Earlier, he had graduated from Jodhpur and also completed his PhD. People of the village held him in high esteem. He was elected as *sarpanch*. Just then, the then Chief Minister B.S. Shekhawat introduced a scheme popularly called Antyodaya. Twenty-five persons from Prof. Manaklao's benefitted from this scheme and derived some financial help. But to his great shock, 17 of them consumed opium and wasted away the money received from the government. Not only that, they were lethargic and hardly did any work.

It is at this point that he thought of opening a de-addiction centre close to his village. Many people from his own village and from surrounding areas were treated in the de-addiction centres. In the very first attempt, as many as 11 persons bade goodbye to the use of opium. This brought a lot of encouragement to Prof. Manaklao. He established such centres throughout Rajasthan and in some other parts of the country as well. As many as 700 de-addiction centres were opened, helping thousands of addicts recover. The Government of India (GoI) recognized his services in 1986, when he was awarded a Padma Shri—a rare recognition indeed!

One day, while walking, Prof. Manaklao found a child stricken with polio. The child could hardly move. The Professor wept seeing the child's pain and took two initiatives. First, he met a doctor friend in a hospital and arranged for administration of polio drops to children. This ensured protection from polio. Second, he opened a school called Sucheta Kriplani Shiksha Niketan for the physically challenged. Polio-stricken children were properly cared for. They were given admission in the school without any fees for books, uniforms, etc. Classes were also arranged for polio-stricken adults. Prof. Manaklao went from village to village, met the sarpanchs, identified persons using opium and helped polio-stricken persons of all ages.

He was working in two directions: opening of de-addiction centres for opium users, and educating the physically-challenged persons. It was a great social service. He won many awards from organizations in Rajasthan and even at the national level. The third highest civilian award, Padma Bhushan, was bestowed upon him by the GoI in 1991.

Professor Manaklao was invited by various countries. He helped charitable societies abroad by explaining the technique of de-addiction centres and sharing insights from his experience. In the process, he learnt certain values abroad and brought them back to India for the benefit of his people. He delivered lectures in various institutions in the country and abroad. In recognition of his distinctive social service, he was nominated as a member of the Rajya Sabha in 2003. During this period, he raised various issues relating to the malice of opium consumption and help for polio, and wished for the government to dole out liberal grants for the eradication of these evils.

Professor Manaklao has now turned his attention to environmental protection, and building healthcare centres and old-age homes for the elderly. He made a beginning from his own village. Lessons were imparted to improve sanitation and hygiene and toilets were provided for cleanliness. The use of tobacco was brought down considerably. He also set up homes for the elderly and provided free kitchen facilities. He was looked upon with great respect wherever he went.

A look at his brief biographical sketch indicates that Prof. Manaklao was an epitome of simplicity. Born in September 1942, he came from a well-to-do family. He was professionally competent. He could have led a life of ease and comfort. But he suffered a severe pinch in his heart when he saw that people were wasting away their lives by using opium and children were suffering due to polio. His dedication and commitment in this area of social service will always be remembered by generations to come.

PALAM KALYANASUNDARAM

Light of India

Palam Kalyanasundaram was conferred with the Padma Shri in 2023 for his social work, at the age of 83. It is good that the Government of India (GoI) had at last recognized his services in the field of social work so dedicatedly accomplished by him during his lifetime. Although he received many such awards and accolades from all over the world, being recognized by his own country was far more valuable.

Palam was an ordinary child born to ordinary parents in August 1940, in a village called Melakarivelamkulam in Tamil Nadu. Unfortunately, his father died when he was a child. He was raised by his mother, who taught him to help the poor and the needy. The seeds of charity, thus, germinated in his mind with inspiration from his mother. As a school boy, he found that many children could not go to school due to poverty. He recalls that he helped them with their fees, gave them clothes and books, and inspired them to go to school. He further says, 'The place where I lived was a tiny village with no provision for roads, buses, schools, electricity, and there was not even a shop to buy a matchbox from. I had to walk 10km to school and back and walking all that way alone can be a pretty lonesome experience. Hence, I had this thought that if I could motivate most of the children to come with me to school, it would be great fun as well.'[1]

Palam grew into a brilliant young boy who was also good in studies. He joined the library course in a college affiliated to University of Madras. He cleared the examination with honours and was awarded a gold medal. After this, he did his master's in literature and history, and joined Kumarkurupara Arts College at Srivaikuntam as a librarian.

It was in 1962 that India suffered a debacle at the hands of China. Pandit (Pt) Jawaharlal Nehru, the then prime minister (PM), made a passionate appeal for donations. As a young boy, Palam met Mr K. Kamaraj, the then chief minister (CM) of Tamil Nadu, and presented his gold chain as donation. Later, the CM felicitated him for being a brave young man. He received his first salary as librarian in 1963 and gave it all to charity. In due course, he set up the Triplicane Slum Children Welfare Organization. His friends and admirers in Chennai also donated money for this organization. Funds poured in from other sources as well. It is to the credit of Palam that he donated his salary as librarian year after year for all the 35 years he served.

He not only helped underprivileged children with their education, he also helped orphans. There was a large number of abandoned children or children who had lost both their parents. He helped them all. His association came to be known as the Indian Children's Welfare Organization. Still later, it was converted to World Children's Welfare Organization. This is because Palam and his association had spread its wings beyond the borders of India. Many children in Commonwealth countries

---

[1]'Man of the Millennium: 73-Year-Old Librarian Donated Rs 30 Crore to the Poor', *Mangalore Today*, https://tinyurl.com/y2d8rsc9. Accessed on 14 March 2024.

were helped with money and material. The United Nations called him 'one of the most outstanding men of the 20th century'. An unnamed American organization gave him a huge sum of ₹30 crore. He donated the entire amount in charity to orphanages.[2]

Palam retired in 1998, and received an amount of ₹10 lakh by way of gratuity and pension. He had no personal bank account. He lived a simple life like an ascetic. He donated the ₹10 lakh received from his college towards a charitable cause. He became a household name in Tamil Nadu, despite the fact that he did not have a penny on him. He started working as a waiter in a restaurant, where he got two meals a day and a meagre salary. This meagre salary from the restaurant was also given to the poor and the needy.

A stage came when he sold all his household assets including his mother's jewellery. He lived a life of celibacy only because he thought that marriage would come in the way of his work for humanity. His work for children's education and for the orphans drew worldwide attention. He was called the 'Man of the Millennium' by an American organization and was awarded the 'Best Social Worker Award' by the Government of Tamil Nadu. He was also acknowledged as the 'Best Library Scholar' by the Government of Punjab. The Rotary International called him the best 'Human Being' of the century. Perhaps, A.P.J. Abdul Kalam, former Indian president, gave him the best tribute when he said, 'A life without self-luxury is one called as living life in a purest form. The Supreme power has graced one such life to Shri Kalyanasundaram. Under his able shadow there are many

---

[2]'Inspirational: The Man of the Millennium Palam Kalyanasundaram Spreads Kindness Like a Bonfire', *prasar9*, 30 September 2019, https://tinyurl.com/5f99zabz. Accessed on 20 March 2024.

who are divine and blessed to travel in a righteous way.'[3]

Former president of the United States, Bill Clinton, observed that Kalyanasundaram had introduced a new method for strengthening relationships between the countries and named it as the Kalyanasundaram Plan. Former South African PM Nelson Mandela said about him, 'The progress of the country depends upon the children and the students of the country. Indeed, it is very great Mr. Kalyanasundaram has been doing yeomen services to this section of the society for the past 50 years and without publicity.'[4] Kalyanasundaram was called 'The Light of India' by Pt Jawaharlal Nehru. When Clinton visited India in 2000, he expressed a desire to meet Palam.

One of the noblest persons with a charitable disposition, this thin, frail, emaciated man deserved an early recognition by the GoI, but that happened only in 2023 at the fag end of his life. But Palam is not bothered about what people said about him or the awards he did or did not receive in his lifetime. His only passion, his only intention in life, has been to make every possible sacrifice to give some comfort to the children in need—be it for their education or general upliftment. He has made unending efforts for the scheduled castes as well. He does not crave any publicity. His only desire is to make the life of the depressed classes and those belonging to disadvantaged sections of society a little more comfortable. God bless him and may he live long!

---

[3]Suryah SG, 'Palam Kalyanasundaram: The Man of the Millenium', *The Commune*, 26 January 2023, https://tinyurl.com/32fs596v. Accessed on 14 March 2024.

[4]'Librarian of the Millennium: "Padma Shri" Palam Kalyanasundaram', *princh*, https://tinyurl.com/ycxx7w2w. Accessed on 14 March 2024.

PHOOLBASAN BAI YADAV

A Symbol of Women Empowerment

Phoolbasan Bai Yadav's story is the life story of a seventh class dropout. She was born in a socially backward family on 5 December 1969 in Sukul Daihan in Rajnandgaon district, Chhattisgarh. She was married at the age of 10 to a cattle herder. Incidentally, back then, the position of women was deplorable. They easily fell prey to sexual abuse and exploitation. Child marriage was rampant, and there were practically no educational facilities. Tribal communities were more miserable. When women tried to raise their voice against this, they were subjected to abuse and humiliation at the hands of their husbands.

Phoolbasan's case was no different, but she was fuelled by the desire to do something for the betterment of women. Her husband resisted any attempt of her stepping out or coming late in the evening. She was beaten up a number of times, but she fought her husband and other members of the family owing to her strong desire for social empowerment. One is reminded of Shakespeare's *King Lear*, where the Duke of Gloucester says, 'As flies to wanton boys are we to the gods; they kill us for their sport.' This is how women were treated in her village. They were beaten up very often and for no fault of theirs.

Phoolbasan mused, 'We have faced endless nights when we

went to sleep without a morsel in our stomach, and realising the pain of hunger and poverty, I vowed to improve not only my situation, but the situation of all such families living around and I tell you, there are countless such people in our state.'[1]

Phoolbasan was determined to go her way and fought against the unreasonable commands of her husband. She believed that blind obedience would lead her nowhere. At this point in time, she came to know about self-help groups. She approached the government authorities, bagged some frugal grants and set up groups like Pragya Mahila Samooh, Kiraya Bhandar and Bazar Theka. The first step in the development of the village was the rearing of cattle. Around 5,000 l of milk was produced and supplied to government cooperative societies. Women started earning some money. This gave a fillip to many other women to join this endeavour.

Phoolbasan then established the Maa Bamleshwari Janhit Karya Samiti. From then onwards, all activities were carried out under the banner of this organization. The work was manifold. A group of women led by her managed to set up a few fair-price ration shops in the village. The message went round and the exploitation by the traders ceased to exist. This was a matter of great relief to the village consumers.

Phoolbasan had been married off at the age of 10, and was deprived of further education. Taking a lesson from her own life, she decided to stop child marriages. Many close-by villages came under the fold of her organization. In due course, her organization was able to stop more than 600 child marriages. Some of the girls

[1]Jamnalal Bajaj Foundation, 'TBI Blogs: The Story of a Child Bride Who Was Awarded a Padma Shri for Empowering Women in Chhattisgarh', *The Better India*, 12 October 2016, https://tinyurl.com/ntjbph8m. Accessed on 14 March 2024.

rescued from the scourge of early marriage were sent to school. Many of them were adopted by the organization and went on to receive their education.

The membership of this organization grew with phenomenal speed. It had more than 200,000 members. A fee of ₹2 per week was fixed for every member. It was a great achievement that in a short span of time the organization had 150 million rupees worth of corpus. With so much money in hand, Phoolbasan and her team diversified the activities of the organization. They launched the Save Water Campaign. She was also awarded the Maa Bambleshwari Award by the state government.

Phoolbasan could not stand the practice of open defecation, and persuaded the village elders to take some steps to prevent it. Women were also made a part of the village council. Together, they first stopped open defecation in their own village and then carried the message to neighbouring villages. To begin with, a block of 24 villages was chosen for this task. Many toilets were constructed in many villages. With the passage of time, as many as six blocks—a cluster comprising more than 200 villages—were taken in its fold.[2] It is noteworthy that an almost illiterate woman like Phoolbasan had the idea of stopping open defecation much before the government initiated steps towards it.

Phoolbasan's work did not stop there. She found out that the men in the villages were addicted to drinking. This habit hardly left the women any money to run the household. Phoolbasan and her team formed groups and sat in *dharnas* before liquor shops. As a result of their strenuous efforts, as many as 250 liquor shops were closed. More than 700 villages saw reduction in liquor consumption. This brought about a great change in

---

[2]Ibid.

the behaviour of the male-dominated society in the villages. In a way, it ushered in an era of joy and prosperity.

The organization run by Phoolbasan noticed that despite the few steps already taken by them, there was malnutrition in the village. The girl child sufferred the most. Much before the government introduced mid-day meal schemes for schools, Phoolbasan and her team supplied milk and good food to children. The organization introduced the scheme in more than 2,000 schools. This became possible because the quantum of funds with the organization had touched ₹25 crore. With this money in hand and grants from the government and the National Bank for Agriculture and Rural Development, the organization under the leadership of Phoolbasan could afford to run many welfare schemes.

Phoolbasan paid particular attention to the educational activity in the villages. The organization paid for the education and upkeep of more than 3,000 children it had adopted. The award money of ₹1 lakh received by her as 'Mini Mata Samman' was also spent on the clothing and education of 52 scheduled caste and scheduled tribe children that her organization had adopted.

Today, India has been declared as polio-free by the World Health Organization. But 40 years ago, this was not the case. Therefore, Phoolbasan's organization took up various healthcare programmes like arrangement of polio vaccination and various other sanitation and hygiene activities. She and her friends even undertook a 344 km march through the tribal areas of the forest and brought about an awakening among the locals about education and other welfare schemes, particularly for the children. Phoolbasan was selected for the Jamnalal Bajaj Award in 2008 for women and children's development and welfare.

Awards came in aplenty. She even won the coveted Padma Shri in 2012. It is difficult to mention all of her awards. But these awards did not flatter her. She did not sit back and relax. Rather, she moved ahead with her work with greater enthusiasm. In 2013, she became conscious about the environment, as forest trees were being ruthlessly razed to the ground by the trading class. Her organization planted more than 500,000 saplings. She was nicknamed as the 'Green Woman' in the area.

She was a seventh class dropout who had grown into a woman with multiple ideas. While commendable, it is often easier for a privileged person to offer all this help and get into media headlines. But for a poor woman like Phoolbasan Bai Yadav to grow in stature and receive the Padma Shri is a matter of great honour. How one wishes that many more men and women could emulate the glorious example set before them by Phoolbasan Bai.

PREM SINGH

A Messiah for Leprosy Patients

Prem Singh is one of the prominent social reformers of North India in the field of curing and rehabilitating leprosy patients. But it is difficult for me to say who is a greater reformer, his wife Malkiat Kaur or Prem. Even as a woman fond of gold and jewellery, she sold it all to help her husband take care of leprosy patients. She was a victim of ridicule by her relatives and close friends for her penury. Prem even sold their house to build a shelter for leprosy patients.

An audit officer with the Government of India (GoI) in Chandigarh, he could have led a life of ease and comfort with his wife, son (Jatinder Kaur) and daughter (Tejinder Kaur). But he had a dream to fulfil. He had a divergent path to tread. His grandfather, at the time of his death, had whispered into his ears, 'Prem, see that you live and die for the poor, the needy and the disadvantaged.'[1]

At that moment, scenes of poverty, starvation, disease and social injustice flashed before his eyes. India had become a land of vast economic disparities; a land where social injustice was rampant. There was acute scarcity of hospitals. Even where there were some hospitals, they were very expensive. The poor could

---

[1]Personal interview with author

ill-afford the expensive treatment and died for want of medicines and proper hospitalization.

But there was a different level of suffering faced by leprosy patients. Prem happened to go to one such colony. It was a chilling and horrifying experience for him. He clenched his teeth and said to himself in disgust, 'Short of food, medicines, clothes and even huts, these patients are dying in large number by the hour.'[2] He came home and shared all this with his wife. She wondered how it was even possible. But Prem had seen everything with his own eyes.

He shared the horror of the problem with his close friends in the office as well. But the only response was, 'Prem, be careful. It is a contagious disease.'[3] Plenty of advice, but no help. However, Prem had made up his mind. The die was cast. He started taking off days, going on holidays or even stole some time from his office and started serving the leprosy patients. He read a lot about leprosy and learnt that it was a disease curable with multi-therapy drugs. His intention to cure the leprosy patients now turned into a resolve.

There are as many as 29 leprosy centres in Punjab alone. He found the patients living in a state of dirt, squalor and disease. He took the matter up with the Government of Punjab at various levels. But nothing happened, except on paper. He knew that he had to exert much more pressure. He had two children to educate and a family to feed. But leprosy patients, he thought, were his larger family to care for.

Prem was born in Behrampur in the Ropar district of Punjab. His parents, Amar Singh and Nachhattar Kaur, were extremely

---

[2]Ibid.

[3]Ibid.

poor. He received his early education from the village school and graduated from Government College, Ropar. A brilliant mind, he cleared the tests for the accounts and audit branch of the GoI, a service which brought enough money to make the family financially comfortable. He married Malkiat Kaur, who bore a son and a daughter in due course. Prem now lived his life with with his head held high. But destiny willed otherwise. He chose a life of social service and thought to himself, 'No service was greater than serving the hapless poor patients of leprosy.' He became fully dedicated to it.

During his service in the accounts branch, and after his retirement as well, he started looking after more than 1,000 leprosy patients in different colonies. His wife and his children were very supportive. He brought out booklets on leprosy and tried to tell people that it was curable. To prove his point, he told them he had cured more than 300 leprosy patients and that there were many others on their way to recovery. He advised people to not detest them or treat them as outcasts. He urged people to help bring leprosy patients back to a life of honour and dignity.

However, Prem met with an inadequate response. He set up the Leprosy Welfare Mission at Chandigarh. It was a non-governmental organizaton. There was not a penny of grant from the government, even though it was recognized that Prem was totally dedicated to the welfare of leprosy patients. Simultaneously, he took care of other senior citizens who needed help and care. A time came when his wife Malkiat sold her gold jewellery and in doing so, she realized that service to mankind was the real service to country. She had no regrets about it. She derived a lot of satisfaction from the fact that she had helped her husband in a noble cause. After his retirement, Prem spent all his gratuity and other retirement-benefit money in helping leprosy patients. He lived only on his meagre pension. He even mortgaged his house to create a comfortable shelter for the patients.

Prem was sad when he had to leave this sacred service for a few months on account of anxiety leading to paralysis. However, he soon recovered. Initially, he was only able to walk with the help of a stick. After sometime, he was back on his feet and began helping the poor patients once again. Humility being the hallmark of his character, he simply smiled after he received the Padma Shri in 2022 for his social service, and said, 'I am doing a duty to my God. My service is like a drop of water in the vast ocean of difficulties.'[4]

The Government of Punjab recognized his services and honoured him for his work for leprosy patients. He was conferred with the national award for courage and bravery by the Ministry of Social Justice and Empowerment, GoI.

Unmindful of these recognitions and awards, Prem remains engaged even today in the onerous task of helping, curing and rehabilitating leprosy patients. This was his dream yesterday and continues to be his dream today. He is a glorious example for the citizens of India to emulate. One often prays that there could be more people like Prem in Indian society to help the poor, the needy and the disadvantaged.

---

[4]Ibid.

RABINDRA NATH UPADHYAY

A Messenger of Khadi Industry

A graduate from Banaras Hindu University, Rabindra Nath Upadhyay was born in a small village called Sarayan, Ujiyar Ghat, in the Ballia district of Uttar Pradesh in 1923. It was natural for a young man born in those turbulent years to take part in the freedom movement. Deeply impressed by Subhas Chandra Bose, he supported the armed mode of struggle against the colonial rulers. However, his association with armed organizations ended after the assassination of the father of the nation, Mahatma Gandhi, in January 1948. He decided to follow the principles of truth and non-violence enunciated by Gandhi ji, in letter and in spirit. Even amid physical assaults from Bodo secessionists in Assam, later in his life, he stuck to those principles.

As a young man of 25, he was unsure of how to proceed in life. He thought for a while and, at last, a ray of light emerged in the form of the Bhoodan Movement of Vinoba Bhave. He went to Bihar and joined the Movement. He went from village to village and came into contact with persons like Jayaprakash Narayan, Dhirendra Mazumdar and Acharya Ramamurti. All these persons, particularly Jayaprakash Narayan, with their lofty ideals shaped the destiny of democratic India.

The Indo-China War of 1962 was a disaster. The calamity

was too hard to bear. Thousands of Indian soldiers died as martyrs at the hands of the Chinese soldiers, and India suffered a serious setback. In such an atmosphere, Upadhyay moved to the Bhutan border and acted as a *shanti sainik* (peace warrior). There, he came in contact with Amalprava Das, the head of the Shanti Sena in that area. Under his guidance, Upadhyay set up the Tamulpur Anchalik Gramdan Sangha at Tamulpur village. There, he spread the Gramodyog Movement and set up cottage industries such as silk, khadi, honey and oil. This helped the farmers with some financial relief. The organization has since become a Khadi Gramodyog Training Centre.

Upadhyay was a man with a high level of commitment and indefatigable courage. He knew that he was living in an area where insurgency prevailed. He set up a peace centre at Kumarikata village. He made determined efforts through these organizations to set up a food granary that could be of help for landless farmers in times of need. This granary came in handy during the famine in the Northeast. In order to help the poor working women, he set up creches and arranged nursing staff as well. He provided low-cost sanitation in the 1970s. In this respect, he was far ahead of his times. He set up biogas plants and arranged for clean drinking water, which was a dire need of the community at that time.

Upadhyay did commendable work in setting up khadi and small-scale industries. He established a weavers training centre and set up buildings, sheds, hostels and equipment such as oil presses and bee-boxes for artisans and farmers. Upadhyay began a peaceful satyagraha when the government decided to oust the refugees who had arrived from Bangladesh into Tamulpur. The government eventually had to revoke its decision and the refugees stayed on in the village.

As a disciple of Jayaprakash Narayan, he protested against the imposition of Emergency in 1975. He was arrested and incarcerated for a period of 19 months. He was a true democrat and opposed when Indira Gandhi tried to stifle the press and other democratic institutions. His wife, Shakuntala, always stood by his side and supported him executing in his welfare programmes.

The Government of India recognized his work as a social reformer of note and conferred on him the Padma Shri, the fourth highest civilian award. He also got the coveted Jamnalal Bajaj Award in 2003 for his distinguished service to society. The Ministry of Home Affairs honoured him with the National Communal Harmony Award in 2006. Likewise, he won many other prizes and honours. He passed away on 12 April 2010 in Guwahati.

What a quirk of fate that a man born in Uttar Pradesh went all the way to the Northeast and dedicated his whole life to community service. He helped the small and marginal landless labourers and farmers, and chose the khadi industry as the instrument with which to offer them relief. He knew that in the process he was fulfilling the Gandhian dream of developing rural India. Rabindra Nath Upadhyay will be long remembered for his work as a social reformer.

RAJA RAM MOHAN ROY

Father of Modern India

Popularly known as the 'Father of Modern India', Raja Ram Mohan Roy was born on 22 May 1772, in Radhanagar in the Hooghly district of Bengal. He was a promising student bestowed with a creative and dynamic mind. He received his early education at home and then joined a *madrasa* in Patna, and later enrolled in the Kashi Vidyapeeth in Banaras (now Varanasi). In due course he learnt to write and speak Arabic, Persian, Hebrew, Greek, Sanskrit, English, Bengali and Hindi. He read and comprehended not only the Vedas, the Upanishads and other Hindu scriptures, but also had a deep understanding of the Quran and the Bible. He was hardly 16 when he wrote a critique of idol worship.

The Brahminical society was up against his doctrine of monotheism. Even his own family argued against it. However, he stood his ground and adhered to the religious principles that he had enunciated. Along with Dwarkanath Tagore, and a few other friends, he co-founded the Brahmo Samaj in 1828, which gained immense popularity. As time rolled by, he found many faults even with Christianity and published a booklet called *Precepts of Jesus* in 1820, unmindful of the wrath of the British rulers. He praised Islam for its monotheistic character. After his death in Bristol in 1833, a letter written by him was published in Athenaum, London. He makes his views absolutely clear, saying:

> [...] I opposed the advocates of idolatry with still greater boldness. Availing myself of the art of printing, now established in India, I published various works and pamphlets against their errors, in the native and foreign languages. [...] The ground which I took in all my controversies was not that of opposition to Brahamanism, but to a perversion of it, and I endeavoured to show that the idolatry of the Brahmins was contrary to the practice of their ancestors, and the principles of the ancient books and authorities which they profess to revere and obey.[1]

Ram Mohan Roy is considered a pioneering apostle of social reforms. His young, sharp and rebel mind perceived many social evils in society. For instance, the cruel and abominable practice of sati was widely practised back then. Widow remarriage was disallowed, and child marriage was rampant. The caste system and untouchability were eating into the vitals of society. The purdah system and superstitions blinded sanity. The practice of polygamy and the use of intoxicants were common among the elite. Ram Mohan Roy was horrified when his own 17-year-old sister-in-law was dragged to a burning pyre to be immolated along with her husband. That is when he decided to fight against all these social evils.

Ram Mohan Roy knew his limitations in colonized India. The East India Company was at the peak of its power at that time. He resigned from his service in the Company in 1814,

---

[1] 'Raja Rammohun Roy: An Autobiographical Sketch', *The Daily Star*, 22 May 2022, https://tinyurl.com/2u6xypcw. Accessed on 14 March 2024.

and straightaway started the work to eliminate these ills from the fair face of India. He had no doubt in mind that this could only be possible by developing a scientific temper among the people. This change could come only through education. He opened many schools where science, English and mathematics were taught. Alongside, he also opened Vedanta College in order to convey the message of the Vedas to the people. As mentioned previously, he founded the Brahmo Samaj that helped eradicate many social evils. He had around him a group of rich and influential friends who helped him with money and material to fulfil his mission. He published newspapers and books to preach his philosophy.

Ram Mohan Roy also cultivated good relations with Lord William Bentinck, the then governor general of India, and persuaded him to bring in legislation to ban the practice of sati. He was successful, and sati was finally banned by an act of legislation in 1829. It was a day of celebration in the life of Ram Mohan Roy. Likewise, he was partly successful in eliminating or reducing the extent of other social evils. His influence was all-pervasive and his vision was so wide and comprehensive that he is now considered as 'The Renaissance Man' not only in Bengal but in the rest of India as well.

In his address, titled 'Inaugurator of the Modern Age in India', Tagore referred to Ram Mohan Roy as 'a luminous star in the firmament of Indian history'. 'Raja' was a title bestowed on him by Akbar II, the father of Bahadur Shah Zafar, when he presented his grievances before the British King.

In her book, *An Historical Sketch of the Brahmo Samaj,* Sophia Dobson Collet, a British author, talks of Ram Mohan Roy as 'a man of remarkable and noble character, who was the first

Hindu reformer since the establishment of the British rule in that country'.[2]

A versatile genius, a man of empathy, and someone with encyclopaedic vision, he breathed his last in Bristol, England, on 27 September 1833. Dwarkanath, his close friend, and admirers who visited England later embellished the place of his cremation, as a token of respect. The Government of England has named a pedestrian path at Stapleton, the place of his cremation, as 'Raja Ram Mohan Walk'. Ram Mohan Roy will be remembered for ages for his multiple contributions in improving the lot of society as the 'father of modern India'.

---

[2]Dobson Collet, Sophia, *An Historical Sketch of the Brahmo Samaj*, Oxford University, 1873.

RAJNIKANT AROLE

A Committed Medical Practitioner

A Padma Bhushan awardee, Rajnikant Arole was born of a humble school teacher on 10 July 1934 in Supe, Maharashtra. His father, Shankar, a devout Christian, taught his son the values of mercy, love and compassion. Brought up in such a healthy atmosphere, Rajnikant was moulded in that frame. As he grew of age, he lived up to the expectations of his parents and did commendable service to humanity.

After his graduation, he joined Christian Medical College, Vellore, for his degree in medicine. It is here that he developed a lasting friendship with Mabelle that ultimately led to their marriage. Highly talented and capable, both Mabelle and Rajnikant obtained first and second positions, respectively, in their class. From then onwards, they were inseparable. Whatever they did and achieved was a joint effort. These efforts are worthy of emulation by any man or woman engaged in the medical profession.

Both Rajnikant and Mabelle joined the rural voluntary hospital in Maharashtra. They worked there with a sense of total dedication and commitment for a period of four years. Both of them were selected for the Fulbright scholarship for research in medicine in the United States (US). Later, they joined Johns Hopkins University, Baltimore, for postgraduation in public health. While in the US, the couple was determined to set up a voluntary organization to serve the rural people of Maharashtra. Before returning to India, they drew up a blueprint of their plans. It ran as follows[1]:

1. Local communities should be motivated and involved in decision-making and must participate in the health programme so that ultimately they 'own' the programme in their respective communities and villages.
2. The programme should be planned at the grassroots and develop a referral system to suit the local conditions.
3. Local resources such as buildings, manpower and agriculture should be used to solve local health problems.
4. The community needs total healthcare and not fragmented care; promotional, preventive and curative care need to be completely integrated, without undue emphasis on one particular aspect.

With this project on their mind, Rajnikant and his wife returned to India and settled at Jamkhed. They set up their clinic in a ramshackle room and over time it became an efficiently-running healthcare centre. Rajnikant found that most of the diseases in the area emanated from malnutrition, water-borne infections and poor sanitation. These three problems had created a havoc. Mortality rate of young children was also very high. There was no proper prenatal care either. Leave alone nutrition, the rural women did not even get enough

[1]Wangchuk, Rinchen Norbu, 'Padma Winning Doctor Couple's Healthcare Model Has Been Replicated in 100+ Countries', *The Better India*, 2 February 2022, https://tinyurl.com/3r39fs28. Accessed on 14 March 2024.

food. Mortality rate was high in the eight villages they worked with in the beginning.

Rajnikant had developed a unique health system of his own. He and his wife visited the villages and addressed the elders. They then asked the village elders to choose three or four women, and out of them one was selected. The selected woman would work as a healthcare worker in the village. In the first stage, their organization covered about 10,000 villages but later the number of villages multiplied and the total population they covered under their health programme was about 5 lakh.[2]

The selected women from different villages were given comprehensive training. The selection was not on caste basis. The women comprised untouchables and upper castes and they were also asked to eat together. Rajnikant was thus teaching the villagers that all men and women were born equal. It is unfortunate that India, even today, has people who believe in the caste system. It can only be hoped that people will take a cue from social activists like Rajnikant.

Rajnikant and his wife derived great satisfaction from serving the rural community. In due course, they cured more than 10,000 tuberculosis patients. They took care of more than 5,000 leprosy patients and brought them back to active life. Leprosy entails a social stigma, and owing to the duo's work, that stigma was gone from the lives of many people. They were very quick to move to where they were needed. Rajnikant considered all villagers as his own extended family. He became very popular. In fact, the healthcare model—Comprehensive Rural Health Project—developed by him was accepted by the World Health

---

[2]Pincock, Stephen, 'Rajanikanth Arole', *The Lancet*, 2 July 2011, https://tinyurl.com/mt9389xh. Accessed on 20 March 2024.

Organization and UNICEF and has now been adopted in more than 100 countries.

The Government of India recognized Rajnikant's services to the nation and he was awarded the Padma Bhushan in 1990. He was conferred with the Paul Harrison Award for Outstanding Work in Rural Areas as early as 1966. The coveted Mother Teresa Memorial National Award for Social Justice was given to him in 2005. The couple won the Ramon Magsaysay Award in 1979 and the award money was used to extend the rural health services. Their organization was also funded by Christian missionaries and the Government of Maharashtra. Rajnikant believed that there was no dearth of money if it was being utilized for an honest purpose.

Rajnikant had always believed that 'the traditions, the taboos, and the social injustices that are meted out to certain weaker sections of our society'[3] were primarily responsible for distinction between the rich and the poor, and the upper and the depressed classes. He was an exceptional human being, and looked upon every individual as a creation of God. He, along with his wife, gave lectures in India and abroad about the healthcare model that they had adopted.

Rajnikant and his wife were lucky that they got to see their children Ravi and Shobha follow the family tradition of service and sacrifice. It will be appropriate to end the story of Rajnikant and his wife with what Carl Taylor said about them, 'They [Mabelle and Raj] went beyond simply improving health conditions ... They demonstrated that health could be an entering wedge into total socioeconomic development. Many... had been talking about empowerment and conscientisation of

[3]Ibid.

people in greatest need, but the Aroles showed it was possible.'[4]

Rajnikant passed away on 26 May 2011. One only wishes that India had more socially oriented doctors like Rajnikant and Mabelle.

---

[4]Ibid.

RUNA BANERJEE

A Saviour of Chikankari Workers[1]

Short of pocket money while pursuing her master's degree, Runa Banerjee landed up in Vivekananda Hospital looking for a part-time job. There, she met Dr Bhattacharya, a noted surgeon. The doctor looked at her and said, 'If you want work, please go and get that patient cleaned and come back to me.' With slight hesitation, she went to the patient and washed her face and combed her hair. The sick woman, who a little while ago looked dirty and soiled, emerged looking fresh. The doctor said, 'You have passed the rigorous test. You can come to work in the afternoon from tomorrow.' Through this job, Runa got to learn about the plight of the poor in the country.

Once, she happened to go to a Muslim locality near her Model House area and saw a woman cooking a big chapati. She saw that the woman divided that chapati into four parts and gave one part each to her four children. This incident again helped her understand what poverty meant.

This was around the time Runa met her friend, Sehba Hussain, a highly qualified girl a few years senior to her. She

[1]Information in this chapter is from a personal interview of Runa Banerjee with the author, unless stated otherwise.

discussed the entire story of lack of sanitation and widespread poverty with Sehba. Together, they came to the conclusion that something needed to be done urgently. But what could they do? They had no money.

Runa organized a health camp to assist the poor, with the help of Dr Devika Nag. However, the women of the locality would not come to the camp. One burly woman, with dishevelled hair, confronted Runa and said, 'We want food, not your medicines. If we have dal-roti, everything else will follow.' This was yet another eye-opener for Runa.

But the real moment of realization for Runa came when a UNICEF report on child labour revealed that there was large-scale exploitation in chikankari work (a traditional form of embroidery from Lucknow). The chikankari workers were paid a pittance while the traders made huge profits. Runa recalls:

> What we saw here was so shocking that both Sehba and I lost our sleep. Young children were employed by these contractors, made to work ten to twelve hours and paid as little as five paise per piece. These people were living in abject poverty. Prostitution, alcoholism was common. Many children were suffering from malnutrition even tuberculosis. The living conditions were miserable and we felt the women were the worst sufferers.[2]

Runa and Sehba knew that it was a challenge to try and ameliorate the situation, but they decided to convert this challenge into an opportunity. At first, Runa implored her mother to give her some money. With ₹8,000 in hand, she, with the help of an artisan, went

[2]Varma, Rajsaran, 'Runa Banerji, the Woman behind Seva', *Boloji.com*, 22 October 2006, https://tinyurl.com/3y6kzek3. Accessed on 14 March 2024.

to a wholesale market and purchased cloth pieces to get stitched. She got chikankari work done on these pieces. But where was the market for her product? She made up her mind to go to Delhi and sell them in the open market. She went straight to Cottage Emporium in Delhi. All the pieces were sold out in less than an hour. She learnt that there was no dearth of a market if the work was properly done.

Runa discussed her idea with Sehba. They came to the following three conclusions:

1. The womenfolk engaged in chikankari must have some education and need to give the same to their children.
2. Chikankari artisans must be saved from exploitation.
3. To achieve the above two goals, they must have an organization.

With this in mind, they applied for the registration of Self Employed Women's Association (SEWA) in 1984. Thus SEWA was registered. Runa and Sehba opened a one-room, one-teacher school. Runa was the only teacher for many years. The school eventually spread its wings and became the SEWA Montessori School with 900 students. However, the strength was deliberately reduced to 350 for want of proper space.

The one clear advantage of opening the school was that the trust between the chikankari artisans and Runa grew. This provided Runa with an opportunity to speak with them about the stranglehold of the traders and the rampant exploitation. Slowly, but surely, the artisans realized the truth. The SEWA started recruiting artisans for work on their own premises. In due course, they obtained a loan of ₹25 lakh from the Bank of Baroda that helped oil the machinery of their organization.

Sehba was always there to assist in the project. A time came when the SEWA employed about 7,500 artisans who worked with great dedication and sense of commitment. There was a rich variety of designs and the chikankari work that these artisans did was far superior compared to the stuff available in the Lucknow market. As a result, the SEWA became quite popular. Runa derived satisfaction from the fact that she was a catalyst in ending the exploitation of the artisans.

As time rolled by, the SEWA expanded its wings and started flying high. They opened SEWA centres in different places in Uttar Pradesh. They held exhibitions regularly in Delhi and Bombay (now Mumbai). Their products became so popular that the likes of Shah Rukh Khan and Shabana Azmi were their regular customers. In a way, these stars became the brand ambassadors for SEWA products.

But this was not the end of the glorious journey of SEWA. Runa held exhibitions in different parts of the world including Milan in Italy, Melbourne in Australia, Washington in the United States, London in the United Kingdom, and Barcelona in Spain. It made huge profits. The SEWA was now internationally recognized as a non-profit, non-government organization.

In the midst of this worldwide fame for SEWA came the calamity in Gujarat in 2002. Sehba and Runa went to Gujarat to help the poor victimized women. Some artisans of SEWA trained these women in chikankari work and, in due course, they were able to stand on their feet. They started making money and made a comfortable living. By this time, Runa had become a name to reckon with. She was a class apart. The selfless, honest and humble woman was nominated for the Nobel Peace Prize. She missed the prize by a whisker and it went to Mohamed ElBaradei of Egypt. She was conferred with the Padma Shri, a coveted civilian award, by the Government of India in 2007. She was by then basking in the glory of the SEWA. While speaking to SEWA workers, she said, 'The Padma Shri is in fact yours. The government gave the prize to me because there is no provision for them to give the prize to an organization. You are the life-blood of SEWA. I am proud of you all.'

Owing to the work done by the SEWA, fortune smiled on chikankari artisans. Their thatched huts were now replaced by *pucca* houses. They no longer lived in dirt and squalor. They had emerged out of a life of poverty and deprivation. The SEWA had, by then, its own building in Hazratganj area. Runa recalls that if she had submitted to intimidation by the traders and if the artisans had not come out from under the influence of the exploiters, all this work by the SEWA could not have been possible.

Covid-19 hit the SEWA's work very hard. Trade and business dwindled, with those involved almost staring at the propsect of starvation. However, Runa did not lose hope. Now, the SEWA is once again emerging as a successful organization and hopes to provide support to the poor artisans.

Runa could have led a life of ease and comfort. She was an educated person. Her father Joginder Nath Banerjee was a man of means. She had excellent schooling and did her postgraduation from the University of Lucknow. But her desire for social reform drove her to devote her entire life to the poor artisans of Lucknow and revive the depleting chikankari art.

I am reminded of the opening lines in *A Tale of Two Cities*, a novel by Charles Dickens:

It was the best of times, it was the worst of times,
It was the spring of hope, it was the winter of despair.

These lines aptly apply to Runa's life. She came out of the 'winter of despair' and basked in the 'spring of hope'. Over a telephonic conversation, Runa was happy to let us know that her brother once spoke of her in a TV interview, saying, 'There was a time when Runa was recognized by our identity but now we in the family are recognized by Runa's identity.'

I wish Runa a long and healthy life so that she can continue to serve the poor and bring greater social reform in the present socio-economic scenario of the country. Born on 1 January 1950, she is only 73. I hope she lives a long life and transforms her dreams and aspirations into reality. I also hope that more women in India can emulate her example.

SHALINI MOGHE

A Woman with a Scientific Temper

Fondly called Shalini Tai by her admirers, all her life Shalini Moghe was deeply absorbed in one or the other act of social work. Her father, Vinayak Sitaram Sarwate, was socially and politically well connected. He was a freedom fighter and had been conferred with the Padma Bhushan for his social and political work. Born into such an environment on 13 March 1914, Shalini was a precocious child. After her early education in Indore, Madhya Pradesh, she graduated from a college in Karachi. Post that, she joined a college where she did a course in juvenile court and child welfare. After this course is when she found the purpose and meaning of her life—working for poor children.

She had joined government service but gave it up in 1944. This is because her heart lay elsewhere, in wanting to serve children. She opened the first nursery school in the city of Indore and started teaching young children with care, love and compassion. In 1947, she set up a non-government organization called the Bal Niketan Sangh. The sphere of her activities expanded quickly. Under the banner of Bal Niketan, she started many services like opening welfare centres in the city and surrounding villages, setting up creches and rescue homes for destitute children, building nurseries, starting integrated child development programmes, organizing medical camps and offering financial assistance for women. All this work kept her quite busy. She selected competent and well-qualified personnel to run these centres and be in charge of other activities. The number of welfare centres rose to 170 in a matter of a few years.

Her attention was then drawn to the neglected needs of the depressed classes. She opened a nursery in the sweeper colony of Indore. Many eyebrows were raised about this. She did not care for the criticism by the upper castes, particularly Brahmins.

Her work attracted the attention of the state government and she was appointed as a member of the Madhya Pradesh State Social Welfare Board. Two backward adivasi districts of Jhabua and West Nimar were placed under her care. She worked with great zeal and enthusiasm and, a few years later, she even set up the Kasturba Kanya School in Jhabua. In recognition of her services, the Government of India (GoI) conferred on her the Padma Shri, the fourth highest civilian award.

When the GoI set up the Kothari Education Commission in July 1964, she was appointed as one of the members responsible for primary education. She made many positive and practical suggestions to the Commission. Those suggestions were not only appreciated, but also found their place in the final recommendations of the Commission.

Shalini had a scientific temper. She was very innovative by nature. In 1971, she opened a toy library. Children below the age of 10 could get access to this library. Toys invented by her were no ordinary ones, and were rich in variety. They were educational, scientific, mechanical and constructive in nature. The young children enjoyed spending time in the library of toys.

Another concern in her mind was the lack of forests in India. India only has 24.62 per cent of area under forest cover today.

Ideally, it should have 33 per cent of the total area under forest cover. Even back then, she taught the children and their parents the importance of growing more trees. She came up with the idea of 'one person, one tree'. The idea caught up and Madhya Pradesh planted many more trees through her initiative. Perhaps, that explains why even today Indore is one of the cleanest cities in India. Her occupation with multifarious activities like child care, immunization programmes, education, teacher-training schools and rural development caught the attention of one and all. She became a popular figure in Madhya Pradesh. She was even selected for the Jamnalal Bajaj Award in 1992 for Outstanding Contribution in Development and Welfare of Women and Children and/or Gandhian Constructive Work by Women Workers.

She was selected as a member of the International Solar Food Processing Conference, 2009, held in Indore. Her work did not end there. She set up a girls' hostel in Jobat. She encouraged activities like learning music, yoga, carpet weaving, tailoring, knitting and cooking. She was selected for the Naiduniya Nayika Lifetime Achievement Award in 2010.

At this point, age was catching up with her and her health was not too good. But she kept working and gave new ideas to the younger generation every day. She passed away peacefully on 30 June 2011 at the age of 98.

What a marvellous life! The Madhya Pradesh government declared her as one of the State's Daughters of Pride on State Foundation Day on 1 November 2011 as part of the 'Save the Daughter' campaign.

SHANTHA SINHA

A Child-Rights Activist

Dr Shantha Sinha is a prominent anti-child labour activist and has been waging an unrelenting battle against this social injustice. Although born in undivided Andhra Pradesh (now part of Telangana), her organization called Mamidipudi Venkatarangaiya Foundation works both in Andhra Pradesh and Telangana. The organization has spread its wings in states like Assam, Tamil Nadu, Uttar Pradesh, West Bengal and Rajasthan as well. Protection of children against exploitation has become an article of faith with her. She is fully conscious of the magnitude of the problem and is working day and night to find equitable solutions.

According to an estimate by the International Labour Organization, at the beginning of 2020, 160 million children across the globe were unjustly employed in child labour. India has a share of 5.8 million in this startling figure.[1] Maximum child labour problems prevail in Southeast Asia. Among the exploited children, male children account for 97 million and

[1]'Child Labour Global Estimates 2020', *International Cocoa Initiative,* https://tinyurl.com/yjsyr55x. Accessed on 20 March 2024; Khan, Sherin R., 'South Asia – Fact Sheet Children in Labour and Employment', https://tinyurl.com/47k68xxa. Accessed on 20 March 2024.

female children for 63 million. It will not be a travesty to term these figures as simply horrifying. When the child is meant to go to school and engage in fun and frolic, they are forced to work as domestic help in cotton fields or in dingy and dark workshops. In an interview with *The Economic Times,* Dr Sinha revealed, 'We were shocked to find out that in most of the scheduled caste families, 20% of the children who dropped out were employed as bonded labourers.' She also said that it was a shocking discovery that nearly 40,000 children were engaged as domestic help in the city of Hyderabad alone.[2]

Seventy-five years have rolled by since India's independence. Although the problem of child labour has somewhat gone down, it still prevails in many parts of the country. Poverty and lack of resources are the main causes behind it. Illiterate wage-earners need more heads to work to make ends meet, and this results in child labour. Lack of education is the primary reason behind this societal injustice. Shantha was seized with this problem and was dedicated to finding a solution.

Shantha was born on 7 January 1950 in Nellore district, then in Andhra Pradesh. After her early education in St Ann's High School, Secunderabad, she did her master's in political science from Osmania University in 1972, after which she went to Jawaharlal Nehru University (JNU), Delhi, and completed her PhD from there in 1976. For her, JNU was a place of free thought, of declamations and of debates on various current issues. It was here that she learnt about Pandit Jawaharlal Nehru, Dr B.R. Ambedkar, the Constitution of India and the fundamental rights of people. She was an enthusiastic student,

[2]TNN, 'Profile: Shanta Sinha', *The Economic Times,* 7 July 2006, https://tinyurl.com/2t2ynmwz. Accessed on 20 March 2024.

bubbling with new ideas. The atmosphere at home, with her father M. Anandnam being a member of the Rajya Sabha, was liberal and one of openness.

Shantha was married into a family of revolutionaries. Her father-in-law, Bejoy Kumar Sinha, was an accomplice of Shaheed Bhagat Singh. He was tried in the famous Lahore Conspiracy Case. While Bhagat Singh, Raj Guru and Sukhdev were sentenced to be hanged, Bejoy was sentenced to life imprisonment. Shantha's mother had also actively taken part in the Quit India Movement in 1942. It was therefore natural for Shantha to evolve into a progressive and forward-thinking woman.

Later, Shantha joined as professor of political science in Hyderabad Central University (now the University of Hyderabad). It was here that she learnt more about child labour and the atrocious behaviour of the employers. Child workers, male or female, were often also ridiculed or insulted. They were also often charged with stealing and lying. Tears in their eyes would fail to calm the employers, whom they served day and night.

Shantha could not sit idle and watch all of this. She founded an organization in the name of her grandfather—the Mamidipudi Venkatarangaiya Foundation (MVF). The aim and objective of this organization, initially, was to identify the children engaged in child labour. Then came meeting the parents and the process of persuasion. The parents generally came forward with comments like: 'We are poor and downtrodden. How do we have two meals a day if the children do not assist us with work?'

Shantha and the members of her organization enlightened the parents about government schemes in this regard. The task, at times, seemed insurmountable. But with patience and perseverance, many parents were persuaded and agreed to send their children to schools. This was encouraging for Shantha and her clan of 86,000 members, who had joined as volunteers in her organization. In a study by Sasmal Joydeb and Jorge Guillen, titled 'Poverty, Educational Failure, and the Child Labour Trap: The Indian Experience', an admirer of Shantha is quoted speaking about her. It read:

> I have gained a lot of valuable knowledge while conducting this research. I did not know that Sinha was one of the first people to focus on children's rights in India. Also, this person is highly dedicated because it seems like a tough task to enhance progress in third-world countries. To conclude, Sinha's contribution to children's wellbeing cannot be underrated. The amount of work the members of the MVF have done so far is impressive and worthwhile not only in India but also across the globe. Hopefully, it will continue to grow and engage more governments to change lives. Such people as Sinha give hope that there is a way to end the horrible problem of kids' exploitation in the workforce.[3]

Shantha and her volunteers covered 1,200 villages of Telangana that are free of child labour now. Children go to schools and parents have also learnt to rejoice in that. She also freed the adults from bonded labour and made arrangements for their elementary education and rehabilitation. The work done by Shantha was recognized by the Government of India. She was appointed as

---

[3]Sasma, Joydeb, and Jorge Guillen, 'Poverty, Educational Failure and the Child-Labour Trap: The Indian Experience', *Global Business Review, International Management Institute*, Vol. 16, No.2, 2015, pp. 270–80.

the first chairperson of the National Commission for Protection of Child Rights (NCPCR) in 2007, under the Commission for Protection of Child Rights Act, 2005, adopted by Parliament. The first appointment was for three years, and then she was given a second term of three more years, which was a great honour. She shot into national and international fame. She suggested many amendments in the Act, which were incorporated at a later stage.

Shantha was conferred with the Padma Shri in 1998. She worked with greater zeal, not only as the chairperson of NCPCR but also through her own organization in Telangana. She bagged the Ramon Magsaysay Award for outstanding social service in 2003.

In 2006, her team persuaded her to take a backseat and continue as their advisor. Since then, she has been acting as an advisor to MVF. But as said earlier, the task is far from over. She keeps herself busy, and in the course of all these years, she has earned the gratitude of millions of parents, whose children now bear a smile on their faces while going to school. I wish a long, healthy and active life ahead for Shantha so that she can accomplish more.

SINDHUTAI SAPKAL

A Protector of Orphans

Sindhutai Sapkal is an icon in the history of social justice in India. Her life was a long and continuous struggle against the cruelty and injustice prevailing in the social order. But she never gave up, and stood up to valiantly face the hardships that came her way. In due course, she came to believe that courage, tenacity and perseverance in a person's life could become weapons against ruthlessness, ill-treatment and sufferings. She summed up everything when she said, 'A mother can never be defeated. A woman can never be defeated. But she needs to keep her heart strong and learn to forgive.'[1]

Sindhutai was born on 14 November 1948 in the Pimpri Meghe village in Wardha district, Maharashtra. Her father, Abhimanyu Sathe, was a cow herder. He was an extremely poor man but was very keen on educating his young child, even against the wishes of his wife. He would take Sindhutai along on the pretext of grazing the cattle, but instead used to send her to school. However, she could not study beyond the fourth standard. She was married off to a man 20 years her senior, from a nearby village. Her husband was also a cow herder in

---

[1]'How Sindhutai Converted Every Adversity into an Achievement', *MoneyLife*, 5 March 2016, https://tinyurl.com/mpn6cc8k. Accessed on 14 March 2024.

the village. She gave birth to three sons before she was 20.

There was an incident in her village that shaped the future course of her life and was a turning point for her. She and the other village women collected cow dung, dried it up and used it as fuel in place of wood. A strongman in the village would often collude with the forest officer and sell the collected cow dung without giving anything to the women. No one dared raise a voice against this injustice. It was sheer exploitation.

Sindhutai spoke up against him and vowed that this would not go on. She complained against the strongman to the district collector and the former had to discontinue the practice. The strongman then complained about Sindhutai to her husband, and asked him to abandon her. The husband gave in to the whims of the strongman and threw her out. It did not matter to him that she was pregnant at that time. Even her parents disowned her. She was left in the lurch. She was all alone in this vast world and had to fend for herself.

Fortunately for her, she had the divine gift of a melodious voice. She went to the nearby railway station with her baby in her arms and sang songs for alms. People around were deeply touched by her voice and took pity on her. Every evening, she would be able to raise sufficient funds for the day. While at the railway station, she found many young children with begging bowls in their hands. She spoke to them and took some of them under her loving care. With the passage of time, her tribe multiplied. She fed all the children with care and patience.

Sindhutai then took a step forward. She figured that if one railway station had so many orphans, there might be many more abandoned children around. As she moved about in the area, she found many more of such children. She cared for them and brought them to her small place, which she called her ashram.

By then, there were more than 100 children under her care. She went around and asked the public for donations. Some well-meaning people gave her some money. Early in the morning she would bathe the children, give them good clothes to wear and send some of them to the nearby school. Her passion for the orphans took many people by surprise. Donations started pouring in, and she was no longer short of money.

Many in the area started approaching her for help and patronage. She brought some children and also some elderly people to her ashram. She gave them permission to stay with her. A time came when she had more than 1,000 orphans.

Word started going around that Sindhutai was doing a remarkable act of charity. Many people started visiting her ashram and saw how busy she was in taking care of the people there. Her mission was threefold: caring for the children was one; sending them to school was another; and the third was rehabilitation of those who had passed out of school. As she was educated only up to fourth standard, she wanted to ensure that others got proper education. It was her passion which drove her to bigger tasks, and she performed all of it with meticulous care.

By then, Sindhutai had purchased some land and built up a good ashram. People often wondered as to how she managed so much of money. Perhaps it will puzzle even her admirers to learn that in due course she received more than 750 awards. She sold the precious awards and raised huge funds. She received donations from national and international organizations. There were charitable organizations from Pune (previously Poona), Purandar Taluka, Amravati, Wardha, Shirdi and Shirur that pitched in. She was a household name across Maharashtra and in some other parts of India. Although an unlettered person she was conferred with an honorary doctorate by Dr D.Y. Patil

College of Engineering, Pune, in 2016. She won many national and international awards. Wherever she went, she made it a point to tell people with a sense of elation and pride that some of the residents of her ashram were working in very high positions in the Indian Administrative Service, Indian Police Service and other spheres of life. One of her residents had even completed a PhD degree on Sindhutai's life. It is difficult to name all the awards she received in this small essay. But a few prestigious ones are as follows:

- Padma Shri in the social work category (2021)
- Social Worker of the Year Award from Wockhardt Foundation (2016)
- Mother Teresa Awards for Social Justice and the National Award for 'Iconic Mother' (2013)
- Ahilyabai Holkar Award, given by the Government of Maharashtra to social workers in the field of women and child welfare (2010)

A symbol of kindness and compassion, she forgave even her husband, who came to her when he was 80 years old. She introduced him to others as the oldest resident of the ashram. Such was her stature, earned through sheer hard work and passion. Her memory will live in the mind of the readers long after they have read the painful yet inspiring story of her life.

SUBHAS CHANDRA BOSE

Champion of Women Empowerment

Subhas Chandra Bose was one of the most influential leaders in the Indian freedom movement. His high stature in the Congress party can be seen from the fact that he was elected as the Congress president twice, first in 1938 and then in 1939. In 1939, he won the election in the teeth of opposition from no less a person than Mahatma Gandhi, who had nominated Pattabhi Sitaramayya as his candidate. Socialists like Jayaprakash Narayan, Ram Manohar Lohia and even the communists rallied around Subhas to make this victory possible. But this does not mean that Subhas did not respect or appreciate the leadership being provided by Gandhi ji. Many people do not know that the title 'father of the nation' was first given to Gandhi ji by Subhas. It was also Subhas who coined the phrase 'Jai Hind'.

However, the fiery Subhas soon had a fallout with Gandhi ji, left the Congress party and found his own political outfit, the Forward Bloc. In 1941, he escaped from the vigilant eyes of policemen placed at his residence and fled to Germany. He is said to have met Hitler there, and upon finding out his fascist outlook, Subhas decided against working with him. He then moved to Singapore. He found the Japanese more cooperative and pliable. It was here that Rash Behari Bose named Subhas as the head of Indian National Army (INA). The INA under his command moved to India via Burma (now Myanmar) and even captured some territory from the British rule. The regiment under the command of Shah Nawaz Khan planted a tricolour on Indian soil at Moirang (close to Imphal, Manipur). The torrential rains and the flooded rivers washed away thousands of INA soldiers and they were ordered to retreat to Burma. Subhas later died in a plane crash on 18 August 1945.

The present profile of Subhas is primarily concerned with his ideas of social reform, which were many. Subhas was only four years old when the family shifted to Calcutta (now Kolkata). His father, Janakinath Bose, was elected as the chairman of Calcutta Municipality. He was an advocate of repute. But the family, by and large, was orthodox in nature. Subhas grew into a clever and intelligent young man. He often visited the houses of Muslims and Christians in his neighbourhood. He ate and played with them, and took part in their festivals. Likewise, the Muslim boys were invited to his house despite opposition from his parents.

After completing his education from a good public school, he joined Presidency College (now Presidency University), Calcutta. It was here that the seeds of revolution, already there in him, started sprouting. He quarrelled with Prof. Oaten when the latter passed derogatory remarks against India. Subhas was expelled from the college. He then got his degree from another college where he got admission on the recommendation of his father's friend.

Janakinath did not want the revolutionary spirit in Subhas to grow. Therefore, he sent him to the United Kingdom to prepare for the British Administrative Services. Subhas stood fourth in the competitive examination. But he refused to take the oath of allegiance to the British throne and returned to India in 1920. After his return, he met Mahatma Gandhi, who had emerged as a strong voice in the struggle for India's independence. Gandhi ji directed him to Deshbandhu in Calcutta, who enrolled him as a member of the Congress party. He led many protests, courted imprisonment and faced the lathi blows of the British. He became a strong leader in Bengal in his own right.

The annual session of the Congress in 1928 was held in Calcutta. Subhas was made the chairman of the Discipline Committee. It was here that he organized a strong contingent of 500 women volunteers to maintain discipline. The entire contingent was dressed in smart military uniforms. They were a part of the Rashtra Mahila Sangh. He was criticized by many old and orthodox Congressmen for this new venture. But Subhas stood his ground and the women volunteers did a remarkable job during the session. Such a thing had never happened before in the history of the Congress. The maintenance of discipline at the huge Congress session was appreciated by one and all. This indicates that the will to encourage women's empowerment was embedded in his personality.

During his jail term of over two years at Mandalay in Burma, he learnt that Burmese women managed the shops, the showrooms and other business activities. Their male counterparts kept the household, did not contribute much to the business enterprises, and remained only passive partners. Again, on his various visits to foreign countries like Italy, Austria and Germany, he found out how women were on an equal footing with men. During his time in Vienna, he met a woman named Emilie Schenkl, who typed the manuscript of his book *The Indian Struggle.* She went on to be his life partner. He married her and she gave birth to a baby girl Anita Bose, who later worked in a German university as a professor of economics and is today known as Anita Bose Pfaff. These sojourns abroad further widened his outlook towards women, whom he held in high esteem. In those days, for an Indian to marry a foreigner was unthinkable. But Subhas believed that Emilie was his 'first and last love'. He had to issue such a statement about Emilie as doubts about his marriage had arisen in the minds of some members of his family.

Subhas created history in the annals of the armed forces when he organized the 'Rani of Jhansi' Regiment in Singapore. Until then, women had been working as nursing staff in the hospitals, but Subhas organized a strong regiment of 1,000 women who underwent rigorous military training, went on long marches to attend classes for map reading, and also learnt guerilla tactics. While opening a training camp for this Regiment, Subhas said:

> Our past has been a great and glorious one. India could not have produced a heroine like the Rani of Jhansi if she did not have a glorious tradition. The history of the great women in India is as ancient as the Vedic Period. The greatness of Indian womanhood had its roots in those early days when India had its Sanskrit culture. The same India which produced great women in the past also produced the Rani of Jhansi at a grave hour in India's history.[1]

The tradition of having a fighting force with women goes back to 1857 when the likes of Rani of Jhansi fought valiantly in battle. Just when Rani of Jhansi left her fort, the command of that fort was taken by Jhalkari Bai, a Dalit woman who was just 20. Almost a century later, the Rani of Jhansi Regiment also fought on the Burmese Front in 1944.

---

[1]Saggi, P.D. (ed.), *A Nation's Homage: Life and Work of Netaji Subhas Chandra Bose*, Overseas Publishing House, 1954.

Subhas once spoke of an incident in Calcutta:

> I cannot forget an incident in Calcutta when we held a procession against the orders of Government and when police tried to break the procession by lathi charges, some sisters made a cordon around us (coming between us and the police), without flinching to face lathi charges. Thus, I have witnessed while in India how the spirit and determination of our sisters have been growing stage by stage.[2]

By creating a women's military force in the form of the Rani of Jhansi Regiment, Subhas brought about a radical change and impacted the thinking of top military commanders all over the world. Seventy-three years after the Rani of Jhansi Regiment was inducted by Subhas in 1943, it was a matter of honour for all of us to read that on International Women's Day 2016 three women fighter pilots (namely Avani Chaturvedi, Mohana Singh and Bhawana Kant) were to take actual combative position starting June 2016. I hope that women will come forth in large numbers in all walks of life, to add to the workforce that is unutilized so far, and add to the glory and prosperity of India.

Indian mythology and various scriptures indicate that there were many goddesses like Durga who symbolized divine powers. Indira Gandhi, the first woman prime minister (PM) of India, was called Durga by former PM Atal Behari Vajpayee in the Indian parliament after the rout of Pakistani forces in East Bengal (now Bangladesh).

The foregoing paragraphs indicate that Subhas Bose, all

---

[2]Bose, Sisir K., and Sugata Bose (eds), *Chalo Delhi: Writings and Speeches 1943-1945, Netaji Collected Works, Volume 12*, Orient Blackswan, 1980.

through his political career, stood for women's empowerment. Similarly, he was all for communal harmony across caste and creed. The ranks of the INA set up traditions of service and sacrifice that brought them popularity and praise from Indian nationals and respect from the local population. Revolutionary changes were introduced only along national lines, abolishing all differences of class and creed. Separate kitchens for Hindus, Muslims, Sikhs, Christians and Gurkhas were abolished. They worked, lived and ate together in complete harmony. That was the nucleus around which the INA was built. It is worthy of note that this was at a time when at the Indian railway stations hawkers shouted 'Hindu Pani', 'Muslim Pani', etc., as if the water was also different for Hindus and Muslims.

It can be seen from the ranks of the armed forces that Shah Nawaz Khan was appointed as commander, second only to Subhas. When the government-in-exile was constituted, many Muslims found a place in it. As mentioned before, even the army unit of the INA that had entered India was commanded by Shah Nawaz Khan. Hindus, Muslims, Christians and Sikhs lived together in a spirit of communal harmony.

Besides the above-mentioned causes of women's empowerment and communal harmony, which continue to evade the nation even today, there are other causes which Subhas fought for. He also warned that unless equitable solutions were found, the difficulties faced by a free India would become insurmountable. For example, he had spoken of the need for addressing poverty and unemployment. He had once said that India had only become poor because the British used it as a supplier of raw material for their industry and further as a market for their finished goods. Moreover, he believed that if timely steps were not taken, the poor and the unemployed living in hunger and deprivation would create chaotic situations in the country.

Subhas also spoke about the problem of education in free India. He said in the early 1940s, 'At present under the British rule, about 90% of the people are illiterate; our problem will be to give at least an elementary education to the Indian masses as soon as possible, and along with that to give more facilities to the intellectual classes in the matter of higher education.'[3] India has now made much headway in the field of education. By and large, people do possess elementary education and some sections of society are so well qualified that they have become the backbone of various sectors for other countries, such as in the software sector of some European countries and even in the United States and Canada.

It is true that thousands of new institutions have come up now. It is also true that thousands of engineering colleges are imparting technical education. The number of IIMs, IITs and NITs has grown across the country. Efforts are afoot to make sure that new schools, colleges and institutions of higher learning are opened in far-flung areas so that no region remains without adequate educational facilities.

However, at the same time, the quality of education in schools, colleges and universities needs to be improved so that the human capital produced in these institutions becomes eligible for international employment, and can bring about innovations and raise the level of research.

It is incredible that Subhas, who was fighting for India's liberation from alien rulers, was also concerned about women's empowerment, communal harmony, unemployment and the problem of poverty. He foresaw that unless free India inculcated

---

[3]Ibid.

a strong sense of social justice, it would not be able to make much headway.

In fact, Gandhi ji was one with Subhas when he said that Subhas gathered '[...]under one banner, men from all religions and ideas of India and to infuse into them the spirit of solidarity and oneness to the exclusion of all communal or parochial sentiment. It is an example we should all emulate'.[4]

Therefore, Subhas has been recognized not only as a great freedom fighter but also as a great social reformer. Many institutions were set up in his honour and he was next only to Gandhi ji in the minds of the people. Even Gandhi ji fondly said, 'Netaji's name is one to conjure with. His patriotism is second to none. His bravery shines through all his actions.'[5]

---

[4]Tripathi, Ashish, 'Politics, Netaji Bose and the "Ramzade" Version of Hindutva', *The Times of India*, 3 October 2015, https://tinyurl.com/muahsk5y. Accessed on 14 March 2024.

[5]Yadav, Yogendra, 'Subhash Chandra Bose and Mahatma Gandhi-II', *The Gandhi-King Community*, 30 August 2013, https://tinyurl.com/bwbcdt6b. Accessed on 20 March 2024.

SUBRAMANIA BHARATI

A Great Poet of Blank Verses

It is difficult to imagine and find many individuals like Subramania Bharati, who earned so much name and fame in a short span of just 38 years. He was a social reformer, a freedom movement activist and a poet all rolled into one. Born on 11 December 1882, to Chinnaswami Subramania Iyer and Lakshmi Ammal in the village of Ettayapuram, Tamil Nadu, he was only five years old when his mother died. His father brought him up with great care and love, and wanted Subramania to learn arithmetic and English and become an engineer in due course.

But Subramania was set on a different course altogether. Right from early childhood, he had a musical and poetic mind. When he was just 11, he penned a number of poems and endeared himself to one and all. The Raja of Ettayapuram bestowed upon him the title 'Bharati'. Henceforth, he came to be known as C. Subramania Bharati. During later days, when he wrote some of his most excellent poems on a variety of subjects, he was called 'Mahakavi Bharati'. This was the second title he earned for his rich and melodious poems. His father was left with no choice except to allow his son to go his own way.

Subramania's father could see that his promising son would grow into a great man one day, and Subramania did not fail him. He became a great social reformer, and spoke against child marriage in India. He went from place to place and delivered lectures against child marriage, trying to bring about an awakening among parents. He wanted all young children to grow and bloom through education. He worked for the emancipation of women in a male-dominated society. He was conscious that this would be possible only when women were given a chance to study. He wrote a large number of poems to this effect.

Subramania was against the malicious practice of caste system prevalent in Indian society. He often said that God had created all human beings as equal. Society and its so-called upper castes had no right to divide people along caste lines. He believed that the Dalits had an equal right to come into the Hindu mainstream. He once said: 'There is no caste system. It is a sin to divide people on caste basis. The ones who are really of a superior class are the ones excelling in being just, wise, educated and loving.'[1]

It is unfortunate that the ghost of the caste system haunts Indian society even today. Even though leaders like Mahatma Gandhi, Bal Gangadhar Tilak and Jayaprakash Narayan also worked for a casteless society, we are yet to see that happen.

Besides being a great poet, Subramania was also an Independence activist. He worked against the British rule. His poems were largely fiery in nature. He was writing day and night for six different journals: *The Hindu, Bala Bharata, Vijaya, Chakravarthini, The Swadesamitran* and *India*. This attracted the attention of the British rulers and warrants for his arrest were issued in 1908. He escaped to Pondicherry (now Puducherry)

---

[1]Arikara, Anakha, 'The Tale of Tamil Nadu's Warrior Poet Who Fought the British with His Words!', *The Better India*, 25 February 2018, https://tinyurl.com/5x7y5e94. Accessed on 14 March 2024.

to evade arrest. Pondicherry was then being ruled by the French. Hence, the British authorities could not lay their hands on him. He continued to publish fiery articles against the British rule even from there. It was there that he met Aurobindo Ghose, V.V.S. Aiyar and Lala Lajpat Rai, who had also sought political asylum in Pondicherry. He returned to Tamil Nadu in 1918 and continued to publish his poems on the sly.

Subramania met Mahatma Gandhi in 1919. This meeting enthused him further and he was determined to fight gallantly against the cruel rule inflicted on the Indians. His earlier arrest, for a period of three weeks, did not weaken his resolve, although imprisonment wreaked havoc on his health. He was very happy when a general amnesty was announced and all restrictions on political prisoners were removed.

However, he could not do much. Destiny, perhaps, had something different in store for him. His enthusiasm to work as a social reformer and as an Independence activist suffered a serious casualty. As was usual for him, he had gone to feed an elephant a coconut. For some reason, the elephant got riled up and attacked Subramania. Although he did not succumb to his injuries, he also never recovered fully. He died on 11 September 1921, when he was hardly 38. A young life that had great potential was cut short.

It will be pertinent to mention that till today he continues to be recognized as the greatest Tamil poet. He wrote on a rich variety of subjects including nationalism and Hindu spirituality. He wrote in blank verse. On the one hand, he wrote odes to great leaders like Gandhi, Tilak and Lala Lajpat Rai, and on the other, he wrote an epic like *Panchali Saptham*. The story of this epic is based on Panchali (Draupadi). It is an ode to Bharat Mata where the Pandavas are the Indians, the Kauravas the British, and the battle of Kurukshetra was the Indian freedom struggle. The poem is also aimed at empowering women in society.

The man who had the stature of Mahakavi Bharati, just at the age of 38, will be remembered not only as an Independence activist but also as a social reformer who worked against child marriage, for emancipation of women and for the inclusion of Dalits in the Hindu mainstream, and as a man who was deadset against the caste system.

SUNDERLAL BAHUGUNA

A Great Environmentalist

While at the height of popularity as an internationally recognized environmentalist, Sunderlal Bahuguna exclaimed, 'My heart is full of anguish due to the wounds on the body of Mother Earth and the miserable life of women. I have dedicated myself to serve these.'[1] One of his disciples, Vandana Shiva, echoed the agony of Bahuguna when she said, '[...] Ecology is a permanent economy [...] Egocentrism leads to greed, consumerism, taking other's share. Ecocentrism leads to caring, sharing and not taking others' share.'[2] This was Bahuguna's philosophy of life. He lived and died for it. Whether it was through his stellar role in the Chipko Andolan, his Ganga Satyagraha, or his long march across the Himalayas, he spread the message of protection and conservation of the ecological system.

Bahuguna was truly in sync with the poem he popularized (written by Kunwar Prasun):

[1]'Shri Sunder Lal Bahuguna', *Jamnalal Bajaj Foundation*, https://tinyurl.com/3crxjsae. Accessed on 14 March 2024.

[2]Shiva, Vandana, 'Vandana Shiva Remembers Chipko Movement Leader Sunderlal Bahuguna', *Right Livelihood*, 21 May 2021, https://tinyurl.com/46hkwe7r. Accessed on 14 March 2024.

Kya hain jangal ke upkaar
Mitti paani aur bayaar
Mitti paani aur bayaar
Zinda Rahne ke Aadhar

(What are the blessings of forests on us. They provide us healthy soil, clean water and air which make life possible for us.)[3]

For his onerous engagement in the task of conservation of ecology, Bahuguna was awarded the Right Livelihood Award in 1987. This award was established in 1980 by a German–Swedish philanthropist. It is considered equivalent to the Nobel Prize.

Bahuguna was born in Maroda village on 9 January 1927 in Tehri district, Garhwal (now in Uttarakhand). After his early education in Tehri, he went to Lahore for his graduation and took his degree with the subjects of political science, history and English. He went for his postgraduation to Banaras (now Varanasi), but left in the middle of his final year in order to answer Mahatma Gandhi's call for Salt Satyagraha. Earlier, he had come under the inspiring influence of Sridev Suman when he was only 13. He courted arrest during the Salt Satyagarha when he was 17.

Bahuguna knew that he was facing double slavery, one from the principality of Tehri Garhwal and the other from British rule. He was with Gandhi and followed his principles of truth and non-violence throughout his life. He never wavered in his resolve on these principles, even though he came face to face

---

[3]Joshi, Hridayesh, '[Obituary] Sunderlal Bahuguna: End of an Era for Indian Environmentalism', *Mongabay*, 27 May 2021, https://tinyurl.com/4aa2m39p. Accessed on 22 March 2024.

with many hardships and sufferings. He was acquainted with two great personalities of the time, Meera Behn and Sarla Behn, and learnt how one could live an unselfish life and serve the public.

Bahuguna thought that the Gandhian struggle against British imperialism was just and righteous. He also felt that the atrocities of contractors ruthlessly felling trees was no less. He was attracted to the mountains. His wife, Vimla, convinced him to give up public life and take to constructive work of social reform. He set up an ashram in Silyara village and started living there with his wife.

However, he was not at ease. Mother Earth was in trouble and he made up his mind to calm and soothe her. He started his Chipko Andolan—the movement of embracing the trees in order to protect them from being cut. *Chipko* means 'hugging' in English. It was a simple philosophy. The loggers came to the forest to axe the trees. A group of women led by Gaura Devi hugged the trees and called upon the loggers to use their axes on their bodies and kill them before cutting the trees. No amount of persuasion and coercion would make the women move. At last, the loggers would disappear. When the Movement started seeing success, Gaura Devi (who pioneered the Movement) and Bahuguna were ecstatic. With the Chipko Andolan, Bahuguna and his co-workers saved hundreds and thousands of trees from being felled and worked against deforestation.

By then he had fully understood that trees were the lifeline of the hill people, and also of the nomads and the tribals. Richard Barbe Baker, also known as 'The Man of the Trees', wrote of Bahuguna, saying, 'As far as I know, in the entire world Sundarlal is the only person who has gone on a fast unto death for trees. Sundarlal is my guru (sic). And the Chipko movement is the leading movement for protecting our forests.'[4]

It was in 1980 that he met Indira Gandhi, the then prime minister (PM) of India. It was a fruitful meeting, as the PM announced a ban on the cutting of trees in certain areas of Uttarakhand for the next 15 years. It was a great victory. But in the meanwhile, a proposal had come up for the construction of the Tehri Dam with an estimated height of 855 ft. It was to be the tallest dam in India and the twelfth tallest in the world. It would mean causing irreparable injury to Mother Earth. The proposed dam was to be constructed on the banks of the Bhagirathi River. In 1995, he went on a 45-day fast, which only ended following an assurance from the then PM P.V. Narasimha Rao of the appointment of a review committee on the ecological impacts of the dam. He again undertook a fast in 2001. This time it was a longer one lasting 74 days on the Gandhi Samadhi, Raj Ghat, and ended only when the then PM gave a personal undertaking for the review of the project.

It is worthy of note that to mark his protest against the proposed construction of the Tehri Dam, Bahuguna declined the Padma Shri offered by the Government of India (GoI). However, recognizing Bahuguna's achievements in the field of ecological conservation, the GoI subsequently conferred on him the Padma Vibhushan, the second highest civilian award. Bahuguna was by then an international phenomenon. He was invited by many countries to deliver lectures and take part in seminars on the issue of protection of environment. While in India, Bahuguna influenced thousands of people who became serious about his message. Wherever he went, he exclaimed, 'Politicians have loudspeakers. But who will speak for the tree

---

[4]Ibid.

that will be cut? Who will come forward for the dying river? Who will protect the mountains? It is now time to hear the voice of the tree being cut, the voice of the river, the scream of the mountain that is sliding.'[5]

Bahuguna became the voice of nature. He spoke for the rivers. He spoke for the forests. He spoke for Mother Earth. He echoed Gandhi's feelings: 'The world has enough for everyone's needs, but not everyone's greed.'

Earlier in life, Bahuguna had identified himself with the Dalits in his area. He could empathize with their miserable plight. He even opened a school only for the scavengers. The Brahmins, the upper class and the people who had power in the area were up in arms against him. But he was firm in his resolve. He even set up a hostel where students of all communities, rich or poor, of any class or caste, could live together. He worked for the upliftment of women as well. He worked ceaselessly for the spread of education. There was a great awakening among men and women. Perhaps it is due to the efforts of Bahuguna and others like him that people in the hills fare better in the field of education than those living in other areas. He even worked for the Bhoodan Movement, and at Vinoba Bhave's call he marched through seven districts to collect land for the landless.

Bahuguna received many national and international awards. But all these awards did not flatter him and he remained focussed on his divine mission to save nature. He walked from Kashmir to Kohima to disseminate his message that the nation can prosper only when nature is preserved. He was of the view that tinkering

---

[5]Kumari, Harshita, 'Sunderlal Bahuguna: An Evergreen Legacy of Eco-Centric Living', *Feminism in India*, 10 June 2021, https://tinyurl.com/mutrh2kw. Accessed on 14 March 2024.

with nature would mean devastation for humanity. His message was received well wherever he went. But is the world any wiser? No, it is not. Many global conclaves with heads of states take place to address the issues around climate change, but for the last many years there has been no worthwhile outcome. Space for survival of the human race is shrinking. Given the situation, the best tribute to a man of the stature of Bahuguna would be to take rightful decisions to protect Mother Earth from man's greed. Let's hope that it happens; when and how, one doesn't know.

Bahuguna, though old, was very active but he was caught in the snare of Covid-19 and died at AIIMS, Rishikesh, on 21 May 2021. His life is worthy of emulation and is inspiring for every person who cares for a dignified and safe life for the future generations.

SWAMI SIVANANDA

An Ascetic Who is a Social Reformer

Swami Sivananda is an ascetic who turned 127 years old on 8 August 2023. He is potentially the oldest living person on Earth. The purpose of this book is not to write on or about ascetics and spiritual gurus. But Sivananda is an ascetic with a difference. He represents a fine combination of spiritualism and social service. His social service covers three important areas. He has been serving 400–500 leprosy patients in Puri, Odisha (previously Orissa), on a regular basis. His disciples converge at Puri from across India and abroad in December each year and distribute different articles of need to leprosy patients. He has given the world a special healthcare model through yoga and meditation. He has also done remarkable work during the pandemic by providing vaccination facilities to thousands of people. He continues to take interest in this area of social service even today.

Sivananda was born on 8 August 1896 in Haripur village, Sylhet district in Bengal (now in Bangladesh). Some people dispute the authenticity of his age. When asked about proof of his age, he produces his Aadhaar card and his passport. According to the Guinness Book of World Records, the oldest living man was a Japanese named Jiroemon Kimura. The disciples of Sivananda say that they are writing to the

Guinness Book of World Records claiming that Sivananda is the oldest living man.

Sivananda was born of very poor parents. As a young child of four, he felt the pangs of excruciating hunger. He lost both his parents at the age of six, within a gap of two hours. His relatives left Sivananda under the care of Swami Omkarnanda, who took him to Nabadwip, where he stayed for a couple of years before moving to Vrindavan. After a brief sojourn, his Guru moved to Banaras (now Varanasi), which became Sivananda's permanent home for the rest of his life. It does not, however, mean that Sivananda did not leave Banaras at all. In fact, he travelled across the country, first in the company of his Guru and later all alone. He has visited more than 50 countries and has a large following in India and abroad.

Sivananda learnt about the holy scriptures from his Guru. More importantly, he mastered the art of yoga and meditation. He still gets up at three in the morning and goes for a walk. After a glass of water, he takes his bath and does various yoga exercises. Miraculously, even at this ripe age, he can still ace a headstand. Later in the day, he sits down in meditation and reaches the deeper layers of spiritualism through the act. He feels that his identity is mingled with the eternal identity of God. Surprised at the disease-free ripe age of Sivananda, representatives from many corporate hospitals visit him to study the functional and structural frame of his body and brain. He tells them, 'Yoga and meditation is the reason of my longevity. I take oil-free boiled diet. I take my meals twice a day with no breakfast. Lastly I have no desire and hence no depression. I am happy on account of the absence of 3 Ds from my life—Desire, Disease and Depression.' In the presence of the doctors, he performs many yoga exercises in a very brisk fashion and then tells them, 'Yoga brings mental tranquility and contentment.'[1]

Swami Sivananda has never visited a hospital for any treatment except for routine checkups. He tells his disciples to avoid antibiotics, sea salt and oily food. He believes that sea salt is very harmful, and that black salt or rock salt is better. He also believes that consumption of oil leads to stones in the gall bladder.

Sivananda has no desires. His disciples offer him money but he never accepts. They donate him houses and he puts them to use for the needy and the poor. The ashram near Durga Mandir in Banaras has also been donated to him by his disciples from India and countries like Germany, England and Australia.

While Sivananda has no desires of his own, he advises his disciples to focus their attention on the less advantaged creations of God. This creation, according to him, is leprosy patients. He has identified a special spot in Jagannathpuri—a colony housing 400–500 leprosy patients. He gives them food items, fruits, clothes, winter garments, blankets, mosquito nets and cooking utensils, based on their express needs. This gives him a lot of satisfaction. He feels that when he serves these leprosy patients, he is serving God. His disciples keep visiting Puri and have taken up the responsibility of feeding and rehabilitating the leprosy patients. This is one of the greatest social services attributed to Sivananda. On the whole, he feels that the world is his home, its people are his family, and to love and serve them is his religion.

---

[1]Salaria, Shikha, 'Disciplined Life in Single Varanasi Room: Legend of "125-Yr-Old" Padma Awardee Yoga Guru Sivananda', *The Print*, 30 March 2022, https://tinyurl.com/3cm5vmnw. Accessed on 5 April 2024.

In this respect, Sivananda—leading a disciplined, regulated and disease-free life at the age of 127—is an accomplished ascetic who has three distinct forms of social service to his credit, besides spiritualism. He has brought the ancient system of healthcare to humanity through yoga and meditation. He looks after the leprosy patients and, through his efforts in this direction, he advises people to understand that all living beings—good or bad, low and high, sick and healthy—are the creations of God and that they should take care of all human beings. This, according to him, is the holiest of all social service. It is with this intent that he looked after the patients who suffered from Covid-19 and provided them with necessary vaccinations and saved innumerable lives.

Life and death are in the hands of God. One can only pray that the world has more people like Sivananda who live an ascetic life, look after the creations of God, and practise humanism through spirituality. May he live longer still!

SWAMI VIVEKANANDA

An Ambassador of Goodwill

Swami Vivekananda's life is like a vast ocean. One has to go deep into the waters to find gems of the purest form of wisdom. This wisdom would reveal that the risky dive was not a wasteful exercise, but instead brought forth ideas like a breath of fresh air in a congested atmosphere or like a fresh spring of water in a desert.

Swami Vivekananda was born as Narendranath Datta in an aristocratic family in Calcutta (now Kolkata) on 12 January 1863. His father was an attorney, and a great Persian and Sanskrit scholar. However, times changed fast for them. The family was reduced to poverty after the death of his father in 1884. Like his grandfather, Durgacharan Datta, Narendranath was also inclined towards religion and spirituality from the beginning. He was a brilliant student with a sharp intellect. His principal, William Hastie, of Christian College spoke of him thus: 'Narendra is a real genius. I have travelled far and wide, but have not yet come across a lad of his talents and possibilities even among the philosophical students in the German universities. He is bound to make his mark in life.'[1]

---

[1]'Short Biography of Swami Vivekananda', *Vivevkananda.net*, https://tinyurl.com/y8jmrdxf. Accessed on 21 March 2024.

After his graduation, he was not interested in worldly pursuits. He left home in search of truth. Many influences came his way and disappeared. At last, he came to Ramakrishna Paramhansa, a great worshipper of Goddess Kali, and became his disciple. His Guru died in Cossipore on 16 August 1886, instructing his disciples to follow the spiritual guidance and leadership of Narendranath, now known as Swami Vivekananda.

It is true that Swami Vivekananda travelled through Europe, Asia and the United States (US) extensively. He delivered spiritual speeches in Japan, Canada, China, Germany and many European countries. He even went to Egypt. He wrote and published journals and books. He propagated classical yoga, music and the Vedanta. He brought the Hindu scriptures closer to the Western world. But one could pause and wonder, 'What did he do by way of social reform in India?' After all, the theme of this book is social reform and not spirituality. A closer look at Swami Vivekananda's life would reveal that he spoke on the necessity of social reforms in India. In some cases, he had an electrifying effect. During his tour of India from 1888 to 1893, he had a close look at the plight of his countrymen in British India. The themes of his talks during these years were:

1. eradication of caste system;
2. removal of untouchability;
3. poverty and its ill effects;
4. religious intolerance;
5. evils of smoking and drinking; and
6. developing a nationalistic outlook and fighting against foreign rule.

The themes enumerated above formed the basis of his public speeches and his household conversations. Even during his tour of the US and his address to the Parliament of Religions on 11 September 1893 in Chicago, he had emphasized:

> We believe not only in universal toleration, but we accept all religions as true [...] Sectarianism, bigotry, and its horrible descendant, fanaticism, have long possessed this beautiful earth. They have filled the earth with violence, drenched it often and often with human blood, destroyed civilisation and sent whole nations to despair. Had it not been for these horrible demons, human society would be far more advanced than it is now. But their time is come; and I fervently hope that the bell that tolled this morning in honour of this convention may be the death-knell of all fanaticism, of all persecutions with the sword or with the pen, and of all uncharitable feelings between persons wending their way to the same goal.[2]

He continued his discussions, particularly on the necessity of religious tolerance, even after his return from a successful tour abroad. It can be seen from the foregoing pages that I have not written much about Swami Vivekananda's religious philosophy. This is because it would take a few volumes to cover the full scope of his work. The main concern of this section has been to bring to light Swami Vivekananda's work as a social reformer. Today, thousands of edifices stand in his honour. This great patriotic saint breathed his last on 4 July 1902, while he was in meditation at Belur Math in Bengal. The Government of India celebrates his birthday every year as 'National Youth Day'.

Swami Vivekananda had a short life span of only 39 years.

---

[2]'Parliament of Religion Speech of Swami Vivekananda – On This Day in 1893', *os.me*, https://tinyurl.com/3ev888z8. Accessed on 21 March 2024.

He achieved so much in this period in the fields of social reform and spirituality. Had he lived longer, he would surely have done much more. But that was not to be. Nevertheless, he will always be remembered for his work towards eradication of poverty, caste system and untouchability from the sacred soil of India. Spirits like Swami Vivekananda are immortal; they continue to live through their deeds.

T.K. MADHAVAN

A Man Who Stood against the Liquor Lobby

T.K. Madhavan was born on 2 September 1885 at Karthikapally in Kerala. His father, Kesavan Channar, was a wealthy businessman. His relatives served in high positions in the court of the Maharaja of Travancore (Thiruvithamkoor). He got his early education at home. Unfortunately, he could not get higher education. His thirst for knowledge pinched him all his life.

Madhavan was a brilliant young boy. He looked around him and found that the plight of untouchables and other lower castes in the Hindu Brahminical society was miserable. He could not take it lying down. He looked around and found a mentor in the person of Narayana Guru. The creed of Narayana Guru was 'one god, one religion, one caste'. This appealed to Madhavan and he became an adherent of Narayana Guru and stood by and preached his principles all his life.

On the strength of his merit and with the influence of his relatives, he was elected to the Travancore Legislative Assembly. He made an impactful speech wherein he remarked that he was ashamed of the condition of the people. He spoke about how the state did not give equal treatment to all irrespective of their caste, colour and creed. Low-caste persons were not allowed to walk on the roads where even animals were allowed. He believed that this injustice had to be rectified.

As a follower of Narayana Guru, he moved from one place to another and spoke to the people about Sree Narayana Dharma Paripalana Yogam. He had many followers. Towards the end of his life, he had more than 15,000 followers who looked up to him and Narayana Guru as their guides.

Madhavan was determined to end the social imbalance by removing the stain of untouchability from Kerala. He gave a call to his followers, who assembled in large numbers. A vociferous protest was held. He and his followers were arrested and released after a few months in the jail. He met Mahatma Gandhi on 24 September 1921 at Tirunelvelli and requested him to help with eliminating social injustice towards untouchables.

Gandhi ji patted him on the back and assured full support. Madhavan joined the Congress and started taking interest in its proceedings. This open support from Gandhi ji gave a big boost to his cause. By an order of the Maharaja of Travancore, the roads leading to the temple were thrown open for all communities. However, Madhavan found that this was not the end of the struggle. Places of worship were still beyond the reach of the untouchables. He, along with other leaders of Kerala, started the Vaikom Satyagraha. It was a sustained struggle that lasted over two years. Initially, he and other leaders like Keshavan had to face the brutalities of the police. Eventually, though, the doors were thrown open for the untouchables and all other backward classes (including the Ezhavas) in 1925. With no ban anymore on the entry of untouchables in temples across Kerala, Madhavan and other leaders heaved a sigh of relief.

Madhavan was pained to see that government service, particularly in the revenue and defence department, was not open to untouchables, Muslims and Christians. This was an act of high-handedness on the part of the Maharaja. It was an act of social injustice and created unnecessary bitterness among different communities in Kerala. Madhavan and his followers launched a satyagraha against this injustice as well. He met with partial success when application for government service in the revenue department was made open to all communities. However, defence jobs were still reserved for the upper classes. Madhavan continued a sustained protest against this.

Consumption of liquor was yet another stigma of society, and destroyed many families. It prevailed particularly among people from lower castes. The liquor lobby was very strong and people from lower castes easily fell prey to this malice. Madhavan approached Narayana Guru for help in this struggle. The Guru urged people all around that they should refrain from consuming liquor. This message from a revered guru was spread by Madhavan to not just the disciples but to all other communities in Kerala. In due course, the liquor lobby became weak and the consumption of liquor was considerably reduced.

Madhavan was committed to the amelioration of the circumstances of untouchables. But as fate would have it, his life was cut short. Destiny willed it otherwise. He died at the young age of 45 on 27 April 1930. Kerala was plunged into mourning over his sad, tragic and untimely death. The grateful people of the state raised a monument in his honour and a college was founded in his memory.

Madhavan will be long remembered for his acts of social reform amid adverse circumstances. He was the true servant of the people who looked after and served their interests in an unselfish way. History will remember him as one of the topmost social reformers in the state of Kerala who worked against untouchability, liquor consumption and other social evils.

TARABAI SHINDE

A Woman Who Stood for the Female World

Tarabai Shinde was one of the most daring and courageous social reformers. She wrote her tract, *Stri Purush Tulana (A Comparison Between Women and Men),* in 1882, when women were looked upon as inferior creatures, and were expected to have no desires of their own. They were slaves to the whims and fancies of a male-dominated society. Her work is a social critique of invaluable significance. She was fuelled to write her tract owing to the shabby treatment meted out to a young widow in Surat (now in Gujarat).

The widow's name was Vijayalakshmi, and she had aborted her unborn child for fear of disgrace and humiliation in public. This was considered a 'heinous crime' in those days, so she was arrested and put on trial. She was ordered to be sentenced to death. Later her sentence was commuted to life imprisonment and she was put up in a Surat jail. The story was carried in a journal, *Pune Vaibhav,* which criticized the acts of omission and commission by Vijayalakshmi. It appeared as if all hell broke loose and the devils had come out.

Tarabai was upset by the attitude of a biased society. It was at this time that she decided to give vent to her feelings and expressed them in her tract, *A Comparison Between Women and Men*. It is a wonderful piece of literature written in robust, powerful and biting language. It presents an analytical study of the relationship between men and women. She argues about why only Vijayalakshmi was held responsible for what happened, when it was the work of a devilish man who had made her pregnant? After all, for a woman to be pregnant is not a sin. She further said that while one could argue that she was a widow, it was not her fault that she had become a widow. Again, how was it that widows were not allowed to remarry? Even the holy scriptures of Hindus, Muslims and Christians allowed remarriage.

Tarabai was born in 1850 into an elite family in a small town called Buldana in Maharashtra. Her father was an enlightened soul. He worked as head clerk in the office of the deputy commissioner of revenue. He even wrote a book, *Hint to the Educated Natives*. He was closely associated with Jyotirao Phule and Savitribai Phule, who were deeply engaged in social work. They were opening various schools for the education of girls.

Tarabai knew that a person without education was like a desert where nothing would grow. But unfortunately, there was no school nearby. This gap was filled up by her father who gave her the best possible education at home. She soon became proficient in Marathi, Sanskrit and English. She was married at a young age to a man who, fortunately, came to live with her parents. She felt independent in her own home and did not have to face the difficulties generally faced by married women who had to go to distant places and live in a different atmosphere with their husbands.

Tarabai was critical of child marriage. She was pained to see the plight of girls who became widows at a young age. They were not allowed to remarry and were dubbed as 'inauspicious creatures'. Their life was miserable. She was hurt about being born in a patriarchal society where men foolishly believed that they were superior to women. She had a strong view that men and women were equal partners and should live like comrades. But this was not the case in her times. This was yet another reason why she came up with her tract.

This tract had just 52 pages. It was originally written in Marathi and later translated into English by Rosalind O'Hanlon. It was priced at nine *annas,* which is equivalent to about 50 paise today. When this tract appeared in print, many eyebrows were raised. There were many hostile voices and many articles were published against it. Tarabai stood her ground declaring that she had only spoken the truth. However, in 1882, when orthodoxy reigned supreme, there was hardly any space for such truth. Her tract, for example, says:

> Let me ask you something, Gods! You are supposed to be omnipotent and freely accessible to all. You are said to be completely impartial. What does that mean? That you have never been known to be partial. But wasn't it you who created both men and women? Then why did you grant happiness only to men and brand women with nothing but agony? Your will was done! But poor women have had to suffer for it down the ages.[1]

She faced her critics head-on and asked them to spell out the wrong in the above paragraph. She further wrote:

---

[1]Prasad, Shilpa, 'Tarabai Shinde: Breaking Caste & Patriarchy Glass Ceilings | #IndianWomenInHistory', *Feminism in India,* 1 March 2017, https://tinyurl.com/4t4fh2dx. Accessed on 14 March 2024.

> Women in this world are forever putting up with all sorts of hard toil difficulty, hunger and thirst, harassment and beatings—and all they ask is a kindly word from you. It's true you go out and earn money, but she has to see to the running of the house, do exactly as you tell her, be perpetually obedient, kept in ignorance and toil away at the most exhausting work till her body's pleasure breaks into little pieces, her bones waste away and her blood turns to water—her eyes always on your face. You've only got to glance at her approvingly and flash your teeth in a smile, and she feels its a joy divine![2]

In the above paragraph, Tarabai gives a graphic picture of the condition of women. Even for cases of adultery, Tarabai blames the husbands who do not give the desired love and care to their wives. She makes a strong argument that to be successful in marital relations, it is absolutely necessary that men and women are placed equally.

Ramachandra Guha, a historian of repute, in his book *The Makers of Modern India* mentions that Tarabai Shinde was one of the pioneers of modern India. He says:

> An individual [Tarabai Shinde] who was obscure in her time and remains so in ours. But her writing, if not her life, compels our serious attention. Her claim to be a 'Maker of modern India' rests on the literary quality and political resonance of the only book she published. This speaks across the decades and centuries and remains one of the

---

[2]Wangchuk, Rinchen Norbu, 'Long before #Metoo, this 19th Century Feminist Challenged Caste and Patriarchy!', *The Better India*, 21 March 2018, https://tinyurl.com/3amzhnus. Accessed on 14 March 2024.

> most powerful pieces of social criticism ever written by an Indian.[3]

The book that he has referred to is the one written by Tarabai.

More than a century has rolled by since Tarabai died. Times have since changed, but not to the extent to which progress has happened in developed countries. Imagine if every woman in India was given an opportunity for education and subsequent development—society then would grow phenomenally in stature. Tarabai showed the path more than 100 years ago, as Guha clearly observes, 'No one before her had so directly challenged the social arrangements and cultural prejudices which underpinned patriarchy and male domination.'[4]

Tarabai, therefore, without an iota of doubt, is one of the most significant social reformers of the closing part of the nineteenth century and early years of the twentieth century. She lived a proud life with her female identity and died in 1910 in the belief that gender discrimination and patriarchy had to go out of the social order to make way for perennial peace and equanimity.

---

[3]Guha, Ramachandra, *The Makers of Modern India*, Harvard University Press, 2013.
[4]Ibid.

UMA TULI

The One Who Stood for Inclusive Education

In my endeavour to find out and write about the icons of social reform in India, my attention was drawn to Dr Uma Tuli. She worked in the field of rehabilitation of persons with disabilities, with a focus on inclusive education, barrier-free environment, medical care and skill training. I learnt more about her through the Internet and watched a few videos as well. Although I was convinced about her lifelong efforts, I developed a great desire to have a personal interview with her. She was kind enough to meet me in my office in Noida on 29 May 2023. As she was born in March 1943, I had thought I would come across a decrepit lady of 80, but I found her tall and active, and she looked not more than 60 years of age.

Dr Tuli is an internationally recognized educationist, a social worker, a sportswoman and an expert in rehabilitation. Schools and colleges generally refrain from giving admission to physically challenged and intellectually delayed persons. Inadequate attention to their needs lowers their self-esteem. Dr Tuli observed this and much more when she was busy with the lucrative profession of teaching English literature in the University of Delhi (Delhi University or DU).

Dr Tuli received her earlier education in Gwalior and did her master's from Jiwaji University. She followed it up with a PhD in English literature from DU. Later, she even went to the University of Manchester in the United Kingdom to obtain a master's in special education. This helped her put her pragmatic wisdom to use while working for special children. At this stage in life, a tragedy struck her family. Her brother, an engineer serving in the Birla Company, Gwalior, met with a serious accident and his leg had to be amputated. At that time, there were no facilities available to fit him with a prosthesis that would help with his rehabilitation. This further strengthened her resolve to do something for persons with disabilities.

Happy and comfortable with her husband, a distinguished journalist in his own right, she could have led a life of ease in Delhi. But the misery and plight of the disabled children continued to haunt her mind time and again. She had to make a choice. It was now or never. As Robert Frost says in his poem 'The Road not Taken':

Two roads diverged in a wood, and I—
I took the one less travelled by,
And that has made all the difference.

The die was cast. The aim and purpose of her life was crystal-clear before her eyes. There was no doubt and no diversion. She gave up her job as a successful lecturer and instead opened a small school at the Brahmo Samaj building on Rouse Avenue under a shady tree. The total number of students was 30. It was a mixed lot, consisting of 15 children with health issues or impairments and 15 without. It was a peculiar hybrid system of inclusive education developed by her. She established the

Amar Jyoti Charitable Trust in 1981. The same is now flourishing with schools attended by more than 800 students in Delhi and Gwalior, with equal numbers of students with and without health issues or impairments. The Trust now conducts a DU-recognized course in physiotherapy. The Centre also has recognized courses of the Rehabilitation Council of India in special education.

Dr Tuli is the epitome of dedication towards the welfare of persons with cross-disabilities. She is a great thinker, in the sense that she always devised new bases and means to bring a sense of relief to people to whom God had not been equally kind. She is a motherly figure to them all. She approaches donors, the state and the central government for relief and rehabilitation of such children.

Dr Tuli was perhaps the first person in the country to start and promote the concept of inclusive education. She was not confined only to the Trust. She went all around Delhi, and other parts of the country, to promote a barrier-free environment in all important institutions and public places. Unmindful of impediments in her way, she moved on with amazing success.

She introduced Abilympics in India. She met with phenomenal success when she went as the leader of the Indian contingent for the 5th International Abilympics held at Prague, Czech Republic, in 2000. Similarly, she helped organize the 6th International Abilympics which was held in New Delhi in 2003. It was inaugurated by then Prime Minister Atal Bihari Vajpayee. There was no flaw in the system developed by her.

Dr Tuli played an active role in yet another field. She initiated inclusive sports and cultural activities for persons with health issues or impairments. To begin with, she organized competitions in her own school and then later organized inter-school competitions. But she reached the zenith of success when she organized five National Integrated Sports Meets, in which children with and without health issues or impairments participated together.

Dr Tuli did not stop here. She worked for the rehabilitation of students in two ways. In the first phase, she provided medical aid including artificial limbs and made the physically disabled feel at home. In the second phase, she tirelessly worked for their placement in good jobs. Some of her students became Indian Administrative Service officers and officials in other ministries. She also helped develop various skills in her students to enable them to make some worthwhile products for sale in the market.

The Amar Jyoti Trust achieved a rare distinction when a contingent of its hybrid (both with and without health issues or impairments) students participated in the Republic Day Parade in 1995. It was, perhaps, for the first time in history that such an inclusive group of students had participated in the Republic Day Parade. Thereafter, it almost became a regular feature.

Dr Tuli's life is a story of amazing success. Right from her school days, she took part in debates and declamation contests. With her fluent style of spoken Hindi and English, she won many prizes. She had a distinguished career in teaching. Her pleasant and attractive personality helped her lead a contingent of Home Guards in the Republic Day Parade in 1978. It was in the midst of boisterous joy and clapping that she led the contingent in the Republic Day Parade for the first time and marched from Rajpath to Red Fort with a sword in hand to salute the chief guest.

Five things, besides many other distinctions, go to Dr Tuli's credit. First, the Government of India (GoI) recognized her innovative approaches to rehabilitation with a holistic approach, and appointed her as the chief commissioner of persons with disabilities from 2001 to 2005. During this period, she did a commendable job. She even held mobile courts, listened to the grievances of the beneficiaries and found instant solutions. Second, she met with amazing success in organizing two Lifeline Express Camps in remote areas of Madhya Pradesh. Third, she published an Indian edition of CBR News' *Reaching Out* during 1995–98 in collaboration with AIIRTAG. Fourth, she organized the 5th International Conference on 'Fostering Excellence through Inclusive Education' in collaboration with the Asian Centre for Inclusive Education, Bangladesh, at New Delhi in 2018. The fifth special achievement is the promotion of barrier-free environment and transport.

Dr Tuli, in her life of strife and struggle, got international recognition as well. She bagged many prizes and accolades. The GoI recognized her services as a social worker and conferred on her the coveted civilian award, Padma Shri, in 2012.

She was the recipient of the Women Achiever's Award from the Consortium of Women Achievers. She has also been honoured by Berkeley City, Michigan, United States, with a special recognition citation. The University of Roehampton, London, conferred the degree of doctor of law (honoris causa) on Dr Tuli for her services to inclusive education. Recently, the Rehabilitation International Centennial Award for Significant Contribution was given to the Amar Jyoti Charitable Trust. Dr Tuli also received the Nehru Smriti Award and was conferred with the President's Gold Medal twice in her distinguished career. Besides, she won the Hellen Keller Award, the UN-ESCAP Award and the Hong Kong Foundation Award for her concerted and unending efforts in the field of inclusive education. The president's office has awarded the Amar Jyoti Charitable Trust three times for the creation of a barrier-free environment, promoting inclusive education, and being the best institute for rehabilitation of persons with disabilities.

The awards are many and countless. Each award has only added to her zest and enthusiasm. The awards fall short of her efforts, and she experiences rare joy amid her students. A smile on the face of every student is the actual award for her. I am reminded of Wordsworth, the great English poet who gazed at daffodils in a valley, and I feel like comparing the sentiment with that of Dr Tuli, who when with her students seems to be humming the tune:

And then my heart with pleasure fills,
And dances with the daffodils.

It's a matter of rare honour for Dr Tuli and her Amar Jyoti Trust that her excellency, the president of India, Droupadi Murmu, celebrated her birthday on 20 June 2023 with the special children at Amar Jyoti School. This only speaks of her reputation and the reputation of her school. Such is the personality of Dr Uma Tuli, who has dedicated her entire life to inclusive education and even today her level of commitment remains very high. Her life is truly worthy of emulation.

USHA CHAUMAR

The Fighter against Manual Scavenging

Manual scavenging has existed in India since time immemorial. This is a dehumanizing task. Village women and others belonging to lower castes rise early in the morning, and go and collect human excreta with bare hands from one house to the other. Their income is barely ₹200–300 per month. The practice is a slur on the face of society. But it continues to exist even today in some parts of the country. It is true that millions of toilets have now been built at government expense, but the problem still persists.

Usha Chaumar rose as a ray of light for a suffering class of untouchables in Rajasthan. She was born in 1978 in Deegh village near Bharatpur in Rajasthan. She was a fairly charming girl. There was no schooling for her. She was hardly seven when she started going for manual scavenging with her mother. This was her destiny. Her mother used to tell her that she might as well learn the work, as she will have to do it once she goes to her husband's place. That turned out to be true. She was married at 10 and moved to her husband's house when she was 14. Her lot was the same. She had to do the work of manual scavenging every day.

Then, one day, a miracle happened in Usha's life. A gentleman named Dr Bindeshwar Pathak happened to visit her village. He collected a group of women in the village and said that he had come to free them from the slavish work of scavenging. He said that he ran Sulabh International, an organization for the welfare of women that helped give them the dignity they deserved. His lecture had no effect, as the women could not even dream of moving out of the village with a stranger.

But Usha showed the way. She talked to her husband, who supported her. She went to Delhi and learnt the work being done by other women under the banner of Sulabh International. Once in Delhi, Usha found the atmosphere very conducive to learning. Every woman got up early in the morning, took bath and dressed up cleanly. After this, they were taught how to make papads and noodles, process henna, stitch, make cloth bags and carry out beauty parlour services. Usha returned home a person with many skills. Initially, her products were purchased by Sulabh International and later people in her own village also started buying from her.

She gathered around her a group of women and engaged them all in this useful work. They stopped manual scavenging. They were now as clean and as well-dressed as any other woman of the upper class in the village. Usha took this message to the neighbouring villages as well. Her hard work impressed Bindeshwar Pathak, and she became a leader in her own right. She became a household name in Rajasthan. She was conferred with the Padma Shri in 2020.

Usha is now the president of Sulabh International of Rajasthan. In this capacity, she has visited many countries like the United States, France and South Africa, and delivered lectures to large gatherings. At this time, her self-confidence has reached its zenith.

The tasks of Sulabh International have multiplied.

It now includes human rights, environmental sanitation, non-conventional sources of energy, waste management and social reforms through education. Usha is doing all this and much more with great grit and determination. She once said, 'I want to eradicate manual scavenging entirely from our social fabric. Women are not meant for staying at home, cleaning dirt and taking care of children. I want every woman to be independent through dignified jobs. That is how we will build a better society, free of untouchability.'[1]

This is true not only for Usha but also for thousands of men and women who are working under the banner of Sulabh International. The organization has become a beacon of light for them. Usha is a rare star in the galaxy who is shining her brilliance upon the people around her and is counted as one of the leading social reformers of today. We salute her patience, perseverance and tenacity in bringing about such a great change in the social order.

[1]Rajkotia, Saba, 'The Story of Usha Chaumar: From Manual Scavenger to Padma Shri Awardee', *The Womb*, 16 May 2020, https://tinyurl.com/yphp7xd3. Accessed on 21 March 2024.

VEERENDRA HEGGADE

A Fine Combination of Spirituality and Social Work

Veerendra Heggade is a marvel of Karnataka and the hereditary administrator of the Dharmasthala Temple. He has achieved what no predecessor of his had, and has diversified the activities of the Temple Trust to a great extent. He has converted tradition into modernity. He has risen above mere temple worship. On the other hand, he has taken up many rural-oriented activities to help the village folk in large numbers.

While holding on to his duties as hereditary administrator of the Trust, he has established many new traditions. He has taken up multiple ventures across Karnataka. As far as the Trust duties are concerned, he holds a literary and religious festival every year where all prominent artists take part. He takes every possible interest in the development of civilization and culture. He stands for the development of art and literature. As per family tradition, he runs the Annapurna kitchen where over 50,000 people are fed every day. It was even featured on the National Geographic TV show, *Mega Kitchens*. He has successfully maintained 4,000 palm-leaf manuscripts in his museum, where hundreds of researchers come, study and undertake research activities. His museum, Manjusha, maintains a rare collection of antiques. It is a treat to see the ancient objects, as they present a beautiful spectacle.

As a social reformer, he participates in another activity of great benevolence. He has constructed marriage halls at six places in Karnataka including Bangalore (now Bengaluru) and Mysore where mass marriages of low- and middle-class groups are performed free of cost. It is estimated that by 2004, more than 10,000 marriages had been performed. Now, when it is 2024, the number must be much higher.

Heggade introduced a rural development project in the coastal area of Karnataka. It comprises 600 villages and six towns. The project mainly focusses on:

1. Agricultural extension
2. Transfer of technology
3. Women empowerment
4. Housing
5. Alternate sources of energy
6. Income-generating activities
7. Microfinance
8. Education and health

It covers around 1.35 million families. He has, in good measure, promoted solar energy projects as well. His push for solar energy has been appreciated not only in Karnataka but beyond its borders as well.

His work in the area of setting up the Rural Development and Self Employment Training Institute attracted all-round attention. The institute has been set up to train rural youth for self-employment and volunteers for rural development. This was established in 1982 in collaboration with Syndicate Bank, Syndicate Agricultural Foundation and Canara Bank. This Institute now has 20 branches where more than 2 lakh youths have been trained. The potential for employment of such youth is considerably high. 'Rural India, Real India' is only one of the many seminars organized by Heggade. This seminar, in particular, was organized to mark the diamond jubilee celebration of Syndicate Bank.

Heggade has promoted educational activity in a big way. He opened a postgraduate college at the Trust campus. Besides, he opened institutes at Mysore and other places for education in medicine, ayurveda, agriculture, dairy farming and such other areas. His approach was comprehensive. He constructed many hostels along with these colleges so that the rural students could come and stay in them. He was conscious of the fact that urbanites could afford education but the rural Karnataka was inhabited by the poor. Therefore, his main focus was on educating rural people for the overall development of Karnataka.

Heggade's contribution to nation-building was recognized by the Government of India and he was conferred with the Padma Bhushan in 2000. Earlier, in 1993, he was honoured with the Rajarshi title from the then President of India. He was conferred with the second highest civilian award, Padma Vibhushan, in 2015. Karnataka state decorated him with the Karnataka Ratna Award. There were many other awards as well but they did not matter to him. They mattered only to the extent that his urge for more social and constructive work jumped to dizzying heights.

Heggade was nominated as a member of the Rajya Sabha on 6 July 2022. Congratulating him on the occasion, Prime Minister (PM) Narendra Modi tweeted, 'Shri Veerendra Heggade Ji is at the forefront of outstanding community service. I have had the opportunity to pray at the Dharmasthala Temple and also witness the great work he is doing in health, education and culture. He will certainly enrich parliamentary proceedings.'

Responding to the felicitation, Heggade thanked the PM. He was happy that 'the Hon'ble Prime Minister knew about the contribution being made by our trust in Karnataka'.[1]

To say the least, it is difficult to imagine and then equal the social and constructive work accomplished by Heggade. It's a matter of common knowledge that religious trusts in India are very rich. One only wishes that these trusts would also adopt the model of Heggade's Trust in Karnataka.

Heggade is now about 73. He was born on 25 November 1948 in Karnataka. I wish him a long life in the service of humanity.

---

[1]'Sri. D Veerendra Heggade Nominated to the Rajyasabha', *Shri Kshetra Dharmasthala*, https://tinyurl.com/3zf96m68. Accessed on 21 March 2024.

VINOBA BHAVE

A New Experiment in Land Distribution

Vinoba Bhave was a saint, a philosopher, a politician and, more importantly, a social reformer. He was a true Gandhian. He followed Gandhi ji and his principles of truth and non-violence in letter and in spirit. His was a life of total commitment to Gandhian philosophy.

Vinoba was born on 1 September 1895 in a small village called Gagoji (Gagode Budruk), in the Kolaba district of Maharashtra. He was the eldest of six children of Narahari Shambhu Rao and Rukmani Devi. His father was a man of modest means and worked as a trained weaver at Baroda. His mother left a deep religious impact on his formative mind. After passing his high school, he was to go to Bombay (now Mumbai) to take admission in an intermediate college. But his mind and thought lay elsewhere.

Instead of going to Bombay, he travelled to Banaras (now Varanasi) where the foundation stone of Banaras Hindu University was being laid in 1916. There, he heard a speech by Mahatma Gandhi. He was deeply touched by every word of the simple yet weighty speech. He burnt up his certificates and other papers and decided to follow Mahatma Gandhi from then on.

Vinoba was looking for spiritual enlightenment. He found a ray of hope in the philosophy of Gandhi ji. He wrote a letter to Gandhi ji and was invited to the ashram at Kochrab in Ahmedabad. The meeting took place on 7 June 1916. He started working in the ashram. He taught students belonging to the depressed classes. He looked after sanitation and hygiene, and the ashram had a very clean look owing to his strenuous efforts. He had read the Bhagavad Gita and was deeply touched by the philosophy of 'action'. In this ashram, he learnt that there was no distinction between the rich and the poor; and the low and the high. Equality prevailed among different castes.

Gandhi ji established a new ashram at Wardha and asked Vinoba to take charge of it. This happened on 8 April 1921. There, the list of his activities was multifarious. He delivered lectures on the Bhagavad Gita to the inhabitants of the ashram. He taught them to live in peace and harmony. There was no gender bias. Everyone was looked upon with respect. Everyone was assigned a role and he or she performed that role with a sense of dedication.

It is here, during various meetings with Gandhi ji, that Vinoba started taking interest in the political affairs of the country. He did not like that the British kept the Indians in a state of servitude. He took part in the Non-Cooperation Movement. He was arrested thrice during the struggle for political freedom in 1923, 1932 and in the 1940s. He was so close to Gandhi ji that he was considered his natural spiritual successor. When Gandhi ji started his satyagraha in 1940, Vinoba was selected as the first *satyagrahi*.

However, Vinoba had no interest in politics. He was not after any position of pelf or power. His interest lay in imparting lessons of spirituality and serving the people—nothing more, nothing less. Gandhi ji's assassination was the hardest blow for him to bear. When Pandit (Pt) Jawaharlal Nehru became the first prime minister of independent India, Vinoba could have attained any position of his choice. But Vinoba was a saint and was not after any such position. Persuasion by Pt Nehru and others failed. Vinoba started visiting rural India.

Gandhi ji had often said that villages constituted the soul of India. Therefore, unless the life of the villagers improved, the country could not grow and develop. Vinoba developed the khadi industry to a large extent. He spun khadi on the charkha and also taught others in the villages to do so. He wore khadi all his life. Most of the time, he walked without any slippers. He walked barefoot while wearing simple khadi clothes. He taught multiple other skills to the village people to make them self-reliant.

But he soon found that the problem was not that easily solvable. It is true that the condition was very bad in British India, but it was no better in independent India. There were big landlords and a large number of landless labourers. Through a rough estimate, he found that there were about 5 crore landless labourers working in the fields for the rich. It did not mean that the landless had no land of their own. But a little piece of the land they owned was forfeited to the landlords, as they could not pay back their interest on the borrowed money. They were now more or less like bonded labourers and led a life of misery and deprivation.

Vinoba had no house to live in. He became a roving ambassador of goodwill in the villages. His reputation spread far and wide. It is in such circumstances that he thought of the Bhoodan Movement. It was a simple message. He would go to a particular village. The village elders would assemble and he would say something along the lines of, 'You are rich landlords. You have lot of land and money on you. I request you to donate one-sixth of your land. This will help me to distribute the land donated by you to the landless labourers.'

He started this Movement in a village called Pochampally in present-day Telangana. In an assembly of about 800 persons, one Ramchandra Reddy got up and announced a donation of a few acres of land. Others followed suit. Thus, the Movement had begun. A village sub-committee then distributed the donated land to the landless labourers. On this initiative, Pt Nehru said in Indian Parliament that the physically weak and unarmed Vinoba had succeeded in the equitable distribution of land in a politically-sensitive region, where strong army contingents had found it difficult to initiate law and order.

The Movement started in 1951 and went on for the next 18 years. Vinoba covered 48,000 km across India and an estimated 45 lakh acres of land was donated to him. This land had been obtained without any coercion or force. It was a voluntary donation. The distribution among the landless was also very smooth. There were no squabbles or rancour in any mind. Vinoba Bhave's unprecedented Movement attracted international attention. He was the first Indian to be conferred with the Ramon Magsaysay Award in 1958. He spent the award money towards the Bhoodan Movement. He also set up the Brahma Vidya Mandir in Paunar in Maharashtra.

This man, with a frail physical frame, who had measured the length and breadth of the country, at times rested at Paunar Ashram. He was getting weaker by the day. Around the 1980s, he believed his final destination had arrived. He refused to take any medicines and even stopped eating any food. He went into meditation. He passed away in peace on 15 November 1982 at his Paunar Ashram. The funeral was attended by a large number of people. Even Indira Gandhi cut short her visit to the then Soviet Union and attended the funeral. Like her father, she was also a fan of Vinoba and his Movement. He was posthumously awarded the Bharat Ratna in 1983 for his unique services to the country and particularly to the landless peasantry.

One thing for which Vinoba has often come under severe criticism was his act of putting a stamp of approval on the imposition of Emergency in 1975 by Indira Gandhi. But he was not bothered by the criticism. His response was that he had always stood for discipline and did not like Jayaprakash Narayan's call to the army and the police to disobey the orders of the administration.

People like Vinoba are born once in many generations. It is difficult to emulate the glorious example of Vinoba, who led a life of celibacy, self-discipline, truth and non-violence like a true disciple of the father of the nation, Gandhi ji.

ACKNOWLEDGEMENTS

I am grateful to Prof. Jagmohan Singh, who retired as professor of computer science and engineering from Punjab Agricultural University, Ludhiana, and is the maternal nephew of Shaheed Bhagat Singh. He inspired me to write about the social reformers of India, including the abolition of sati by Raja Ram Mohan Roy in 1829.

I owe a debt of gratitude to the Prime Minister's Museum & Library as also to the National Archives of India, New Delhi, for lending me adequate support. I am thankful to Smt. Kusum Karki who browsed the Internet and made substantial material available in the form of biographical sketches, and articles on or by the concerned social reformers.

I am also thankful to the members of my family, particularly my sons Vikram and Vivek, who supported me all through this arduous task.

I am thankful to Rupa Publications for their meticulous care in the publication of this book.

BIBLIOGRAPHY

'Brief History of Mitraniketan', *Mitraniketan.org,* https://tinyurl.com/5cmnryv8. Accessed on 7 July 2023.

'Daya Bai', *Nettv4u,* https://tinyurl.com/4ff37re4. Accessed on 25 April 2023.

'E V Ramasamy "Periyar"', *Vajiram & Ravi,* 27 December 2019, https://tinyurl.com/ywvd8zbe. Accessed on 28 June 2023.

'Human Rights: The Birthright of Humanity', *The UNESCO Courier,* 13 February 2018, https://tinyurl.com/ns6fuv8n. Accessed on 2 May 2023.

'Kailash Satyarthi: Nobel Lecture', *The Nobel Prize,* https://tinyurl.com/yu3xkarz. Accessed on 2 May 2023.

'Kerala: Social Activist Daya Bai Refuses to End Fast, Seeks Written Assurance', *The Times of India,* 17 October 2022, https://tinyurl.com/eajhtcys. Accessed on 28 April 2023.

'Social Reformer of 21st Century - Shantha Sinha', *SlideShare,* https://tinyurl.com/4hnks9dw. Accessed on 28 June 2023.

Anand, Reema, *His Sacred Burden: The Life of Bhagat Puran Singh,* Penguin Random House India, 2004.

Badrinath, Chaturvedi, *Swami Vivekananda: The Living Vedanta,* Penguin, 2015.

Bajaj, Jankidevi, *My Life's Journey,* Aico Publishing House, 2019.

Chatterjee, Aroup, *Mother Teresa: The Untold Story,*Fingerprint! Publishing, 2016.

Deshmukh, Durgabai, *Chintaman and I,* Allied Publishers, 1980.

Dobson Collet, Sophia, *An Historical Sketch of The Brahmo Samaj,* Calcutta Central Press Company Ltd., 1873.

Dr. Babasaheb Ambedkar: Writings and Speeches, Dr. Ambedkar Foundation, 2014.

Guha, Ramachandra, *Makers of Modern India,* Harvard University Press, 2013.

Guha, Ramachandra, *Raja Rammohan Roy: The First Liberal of India,* Penguin Random House India, 2018.

Husain, Marziyah, '10 Women Social Reformers Who Fought to Bring Change in India', *YourStory,* 24 June 2016, https://tinyurl.com/2epemycj. Accessed on 28 June 2023.

James, George Alfred, *Ecology Is Permanent Economy: The Activism and Environmental Philosophy of Sunderlal Bahuguna,* State University of New York Press, 2013.

Kainthla, Anita, *Baba Amte: A Biography,* Viva Books, 2005.

Kak, Ushi, *Idris & Bilkees Latif: The Fragrance Lingers On,* KW Publishers, 2019.

Kumar, Pradeep, 'Indian Women Social Reformers Who Catapulted Social Changes', *Arunachal Observer,* 21 August 2019, https://tinyurl.com/2ymemx34. Accessed on28 June 2023.

Lambert-Hurley, Siobhan, *Muslim Women, Reform and Princely Patronage: Nawab Sultan Jahan Begam of Bhopal,* Taylor & Francis, 2006.

Mohan Rao,U.S., *Pen-Portraits and Tributes by Gandhiji,* National Book Trust, 1969.

Rao, Y. Ravindranath, *Bindeshwar Pathak: A Social Reformer,* Rupa Publications, 2021.

Roy Chaudhury, P.C., *Gandhi and His Contemporaries,* Sterling Publishers, 1972.

Roy, Arundhati, *The Doctor and the Saint: The Ambedkar-Gandhi Debate: Caste, Race and Annihilation of Caste,* Penguin Random House India, 2019.

Singh, Manoj K., *Pandit Madan Mohan Malviya,* Kaushik Publishing House, 2020.

Trivedi, Tanuja, *Dayanand Saraswati: His Life and Ideas,* Jnanada Prakashan, 2012.

Vas, E.A., *Subhas Chandra Bose: The Man and His Times,* Lancer Publishers, 2008.

Williams, Melwyn, 'Daya Bai the Textbook of Mercy ! A Life Extraordinaire: Love Sans Borders', *WFY,* 31 October 2022, https://tinyurl.com/yhc6p7b3. Accessed on 28 April 2023.

www.ingramcontent.com/pod-product-compliance
Lightning Source LLC
La Vergne TN
LVHW100525110826
845146LV00002B/776

* 9 7 8 9 3 6 1 5 6 7 7 3 5 *